365 WONDERS of the WORLD

Reprinted in 2018

An imprint of Om Books International

Corporate & Editorial Office
A 12, Sector 64, Noida 201 301
Uttar Pradesh, India
Phone: +91 120 477 4100
Email: editorial@ombooks.com
Website: www.ombooksinternational.com

Sales Office
107, Ansari Road, Darya Ganj, New Delhi 110 002, India
Phone: +91 11 4000 9000
Fax: +91 11 2327 8091
Email: sales@ombooks.com
Website: www.ombooks.com

ISBN: 978-93-80069-35-7

Printed in India

1 0 9 8 7 6 5

365 WONDERS of the WORLD

Om
KIDZ
An imprint of Om Books International

Contents

MARCH

FEBRUARY

🎺 MAY

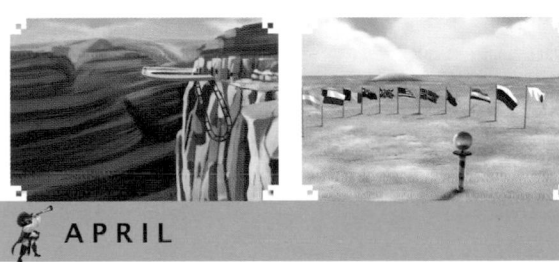

🎺 APRIL

JUNE

JULY

AUGUST

OCTOBER

SEPTEMBER

DECEMBER

NOVEMBER

Did You Know?

- The construction of the Taj Mahal took 22 years, from 1632 to 1654. A workforce of 20,000 artisans was brought from many places for building the Taj Mahal.
- The Great Barrier Reef is the only living thing on Earth visible from space.

1 TAJ MAHAL

This brilliant piece of Mughal architecture is situated in Agra, India, on the southern bank of the River Yamuna. The Taj Mahal was designated a UNESCO World Heritage site in 1983. It is also one of the new Seven Wonders of the World. The Taj Mahal is a mausoleum (burial place).

It was built by the Mughal emperor Shah Jahan (1628–1658) in the memory of his beloved wife, Mumtaz Mahal.

The construction of the Taj Mahal took 22 years, from 1632 to 1654. More than 20,000 workers were employed. The material was brought in from all over India and Central Asia and it took a fleet of 1,000 elephants to transport it to the site. About ₹ 32 crore were spent during the construction of the monument.

The Taj Mahal stands on a square marble base, 312 feet on each side, and 23 feet high. The building is a square of

186 feet on each side. Atop the entire building is a large onion-shaped dome. It is supported on a tall drum, and the top stands 243 feet above garden level. There are parapets over each arch. Much of the decoration, apart from geometrical designs, consists of verses from the Koran written on the marble. The Taj sparkles in the moonlight when the semiprecious stones in the white marble on the main mausoleum catch the glow of the moon. It is said that the Taj is pinkish in the morning, milky white in the evening and golden when the moon shines.

2 GOLDEN GATE BRIDGE

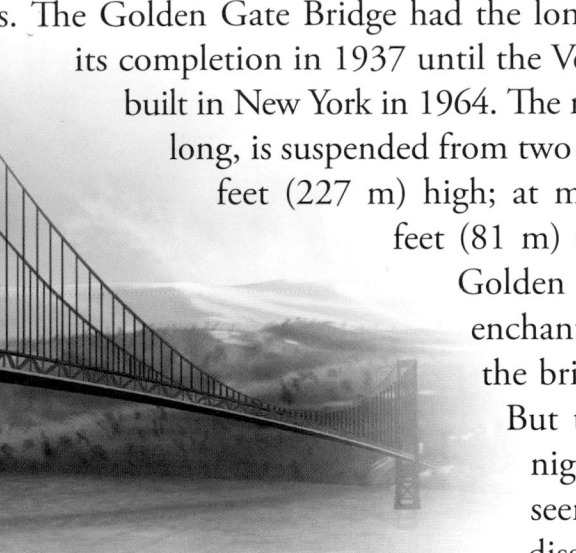

The Golden Gate Bridge is in San Francisco, U.S. It was designed by engineer Joseph Strauss. The Golden Gate Bridge had the longest span in the world from its completion in 1937 until the Verrazano Narrows Bridge was built in New York in 1964. The main span 4200 feet (1280 m) long, is suspended from two cables hung from towers 746 feet (227 m) high; at midpoint the roadway is 265 feet (81 m) above mean high water. The Golden Gate Bridge is at its most enchanting in the morning when the bridge is often covered in mist. But the bridge is also alluring at night when the lighting makes it seem as if the spires of the towers dissolve in the darkness.

3 ABU SIMBEL

Abu Simbel is also known as Abu Sunbul. It is in southern Egypt along the River Nile about 290 kilometres southwest of Aswan. It is a site of two temples built by Egyptian King Ramses II. The temples were carved out of a sandstone cliff on the west bank of the River Nile. The temples were shifted to higher ground in the 1960s as the waters of Lake Nasser began to rise following completion of the Aswan High Dam. This was considered a great engineering feat. A very good Sound and Light show has been introduced at Abu Simbel in the evening. This includes projections onto the two temples showing how they once would have looked. It is part of the UNESCO World Heritage Site of 'Nubian Monuments'.

4 TIERRA DEL FUEGO

Tierra del Fuego was formerly the name given to the lands south of the Straits of Magellan. About two-thirds of the island group belongs to Chile and the rest to Argentina. It was Ferdinand Magellan who while sailing around the tip of South America in 1520 observed many fires lit by Indians along the coast. He called the land Tierra del Fuego or '*Land of Fire*.' The total land area of these islands is 28,473 square miles (73,745 sq km).

5 GALÁPAGOS ISLANDS

The Galápagos Islands are in the Pacific Ocean some 1000 kilometres from the South American continent. Nine islands and about 50 islets and reefs are scattered over an area of about 200 miles (320 km) in diameter. Located at the confluence of three ocean currents, the Galápagos are a 'melting pot' of marine species. Giant tortoises were once so abundant that Spanish explorers named the islands after them, from the Spanish word *galápago* meaning 'tortoise.' It is listed as a UNESCO World Heritage Site.

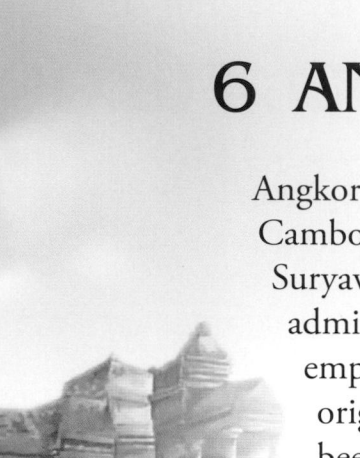

6 ANGKOR WAT

Angkor Wat is situated in Angkor, Cambodia. It was built by King Suryavarman II as a temple and administrative centre for his empire. The designs in the original construction have been derived from Hinduism. The temple was dedicated to the Hindu Trinity Shiva, Brahma and Vishnu. In Angkor Wat, the five central towers symbolise the peaks of the mountain. The temple walls are covered with bas-relief sculptures of very high quality, representing Hindu gods and ancient Khmer scenes. The Angkor Wat complex was mysteriously abandoned in the early 15th century and was rediscovered in the late 19th century. It is listed as a UNESCO World Heritage Site.

7 EASTER ISLAND

Easter Island is one of the most isolated islands in the world. It is situated in the South Pacific Ocean, about 2,350 miles west of Chile. The island was called Rapa Nui by the inhabitants. The name 'Easter Island' was given by a Dutch explorer who discovered it on Easter Sunday in 1722. There are more than 600 huge statues called 'mo'ai' spread over the island, each carved from a single block of soft stone by the Rapa Nui people. Some are more than 30 feet (9 m) high. The island was made into a national park in 1935. It is listed as a UNESCO World Heritage Site.

8 CHARTRES CATHEDRAL

This cathedral is located in the town of Chartres in northwestern France. It marks the high point of French Gothic art. It is built of limestone. It stands some 112 feet (34 m) high and is 427 feet (130 m) long. It is well known for its architecture and numerous sculptures and its stained glass. It has 176 stained-glass windows. In 1979, Chartres Cathedral was designated a UNESCO World Heritage Site.

9 COLOSSUS OF RHODES

The Colossus of Rhodes was a huge statue of the Sun God Helios in Rhodes, Greece, in the 3rd century BC. It was one of the Seven Wonders of the Ancient World. It was carved by Chares of Lindos. Legend has it that the 100–125 feet-high statue stood astride the harbour and ships sailed between its legs. Having stood for nearly 70 years, it was destroyed by an earthquake in 226 BC.

10 STONEHENGE

Stonehenge was built between 3100 and 1550 BC about 8 miles (13 km) north of Salisbury, England. It is a circular group of huge, erect stones. Stonehenge is probably the most important prehistoric monument in the whole of Britain and has attracted visitors from very early times.

There were three main periods of building: the first period beginning around 3100 BC included the digging of a circular ditch and a ring of 56 pits, known as Aubrey Holes.

In the second period, around 2100 BC, huge pillars of rock were brought from southwestern Wales and erected in two concentric circles around the centre of the site. The double circle was never completed and was dismantled during the following period. The monument was remodelled in the third period. A circle of 30 upright stones weighing up to 50 tons each was erected and capped by a ring of stone lintels. These enclosed a horseshoe-shaped formation of five pairs of upright stones, each pair capped with a stone lintel. This final phase of building probably ended before 1500 BC.

Scientists believe that early people were able to foretell eclipses of the sun and the moon by the positions of these celestial bodies in relation to the stone monument. The site may have served as an observatory where early rituals or religious ceremonies took place on specific days of the year.

11 MATTERHORN

The Matterhorn is a classic peak, a sharp, isolated rock pyramid with steep narrow ridges jutting from the surrounding glaciers. It is located near the Swiss-Italian border, 6 miles (10 km) southwest of Zermatt, Switzerland. The mountain is 14,691 feet (4,478 m) high, and its peak dominates the town of Zermatt as well as the surrounding area. The Matterhorn is in the central range of the Alps known as the Pennine Alps. Approximately 3,000 experienced climbers attempt the Matterhorn each summer. 'Matterhorn', the Swiss name, is derived from the Swiss word *matte*, meaning 'meadow'. It means 'Mountain or Peak of the Meadows'.

12 NEMRUT DAG

At the top of Mount Nemrut, King Antiochus I (69–34 BC) of Commagene built his tomb-sanctuary along with huge statues (8–9 metres high) of himself, two lions and two eagles, and various Greek and Persian gods such as Hercules, Zeus, Tyche and Apollo-Mithras in 62 BC. The heads of the statues are scattered throughout the site. There are stone slabs, with bas-relief figures on them that are thought to have formed a large wall painting. It is designated a UNESCO World Heritage Site.

13 DEAD SEA

The Dead Sea lies between Israel and Jordan. Its basin lies some 1,300 feet (400 m) below sea level, making it the lowest body of water in the world. The lake is about 50 miles (80 km) long and 11 miles (18 km) wide. Its surface area is about 394 square miles (1,020 sq km). The Dead Sea is the world's saltiest natural lake. Its near-surface waters are more than eight times as saline as the ocean and the lake's salt concentration increases with depth. The extreme salinity allows humans to float easily, but it prevents all living things except bacteria from inhabiting the lake.

It is known in the Bible as the 'Salt Sea' or the 'Sea of the Arabah'. It is named so because its high mineral content allows nothing to live in its waters. Other post-Biblical names for the Dead Sea include the 'Sea of Sodom,' the 'Sea of Lot,' the 'Sea of Asphalt' and the 'Stinking Sea.'

The Dead Sea is rich in minerals including salt, potash, bromides and bitumen, or native asphalt.

Temperatures at the Dead Sea are very hot in summer and mild in winter.

14 BRITISH MUSEUM

The British Museum is in London, England. There are approximately 7 million objects in the museum. Among the British Museum's most famous holdings are the Elgin Marbles, consisting mainly of architectural fragments from the Parthenon at Athens; Greek sculptures from the Mausoleum of Halicarnassus and from the Temple of Artemis at Ephesus; the Rosetta Stone, which provided the key to reading ancient Egyptian hieroglyphic script; the Black Obelisk and other Assyrian relics from the palace and temples at Calah and Nineveh.

15 FORBIDDEN CITY

The Forbidden City, also named Palace Museum, is the most magnificent and splendid palace complex in China. It is situated in the Tiananmen Square in Beijing. The palaces of 24 of the Ming and Qing emperors are behind a maze of golden tiled roofs and dark red walls. Covering an area of 720,000 square metres, it is the largest imperial palace complex in the world. The city was declared a UNESCO World Heritage Site in 1987.

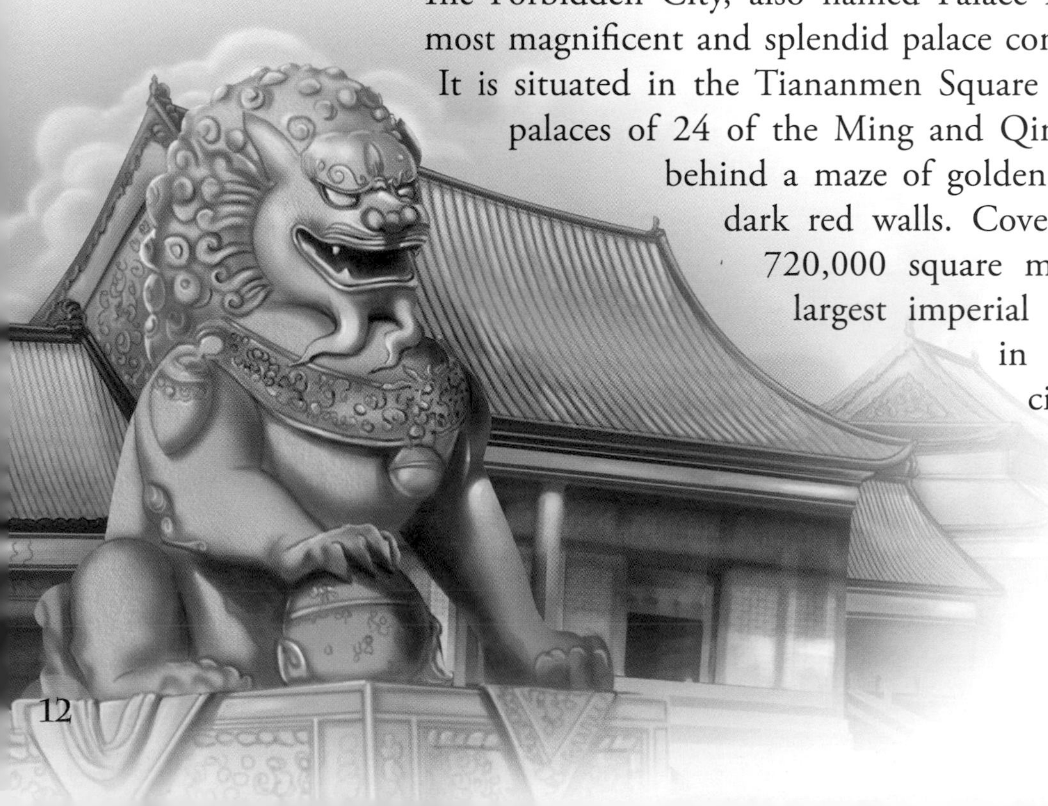

16 WINDSOR CASTLE

Windsor Castle is the largest inhabited castle in the world. The castle is the residence of the British royal family at Windsor, about 22 miles (35 km) west of London. It stands on a chalk cliff above the River Thames near the small town of Windsor. The site of the castle occupies 13 acres (5.26 ha).

The castle also features Queen Mary's Dolls' House, the most famous dolls' house in the world.

The Changing of the Guard is one of the highlights of a visit to Windsor. A band usually accompanies the Guards, although this is subject to weather conditions.

17 BROOKLYN BRIDGE

Brooklyn Bridge was originally called the East River Bridge. It was constructed between 1869 and 1883. The bridge spans the East River in New York City, connecting Manhattan and Brooklyn. It was the first cable-wire steel suspension bridge in the world and was 1595 feet (486 m) long. John Augustus Roebling designed it.

18 BIG BEN

Big Ben is one of London's best-known landmarks. It looks most spectacular at night when the clock faces are illuminated.

The four dials of the clock are 23 square feet, the minute hand is 14 feet long and the figures are 2 feet high.

The name Big Ben actually refers not to the clock tower itself, but to the thirteen ton bell hung within. The bell was named after the first commissioner of works, Sir Benjamin Hall.

The clock tower was completed in 1859 and the Great Clock started on May 31, with the Great Bell first struck time on July 11 and the quarter bells first chimed on September 7.

19 MOUNT RUSHMORE NATIONAL MEMORIAL

Mount Rushmore National Memorial is a huge mountain sculpture of the four U.S. presidents, located near Keystone, in the Black Hills of South Dakota. The presidents depicted are George Washington, Thomas Jefferson, Theodore Roosevelt and Abraham Lincoln. The work was designed by the sculptor John Gutzon Borglum (1871–1941). The four heads represent, respectively, the nation's independence, democratic process, leadership in world affairs, and equality. Each sculpture is about 60-feet (18 m) tall.

20 REICHSTAG

The Reichstag, the seat of the German Parliament, is one of Berlin's most historical landmarks. Paul Wallot, a German architect, designed this imposing Neo-Renaissance building, 137 metres long and 97 metres wide (450 ft 318 ft). The building was constructed between 1884 and 1894. In 1933, a fire broke out in the building, destroying much of the Reichstag. By the 1970s, it had undergone partial restoration and became a museum of German history. More extensive restoration and renovation took place, under the direction of the British architect Sir Norman Foster in 1990, and the building's huge glass dome, once its most recognisable feature, was rebuilt.

21 CANARY ISLANDS

The Canary Islands lie in the Atlantic Ocean about 60 miles (95 km) from the northwest coast of Africa. Their total area is 2893 square miles (7,492 sq km). The name 'Canary' is derived from 'canis', the Latin word for 'dog'. Early explorers named them after the many dogs they found there. The Canary Islands comprise seven principal islands—Tenerife, Gran Canaria, La Palma, Hierro, Gomera, Lanzarote, and Fuerteventura—and several smaller uninhabited ones. The Canary Islands are volcanic in origin.

22 KATHMANDU VALLEY

Of the ten UNESCO World Heritage Sites in Nepal, seven cultural heritage sites are in the Kathmandu Valley. The seven include the Durbar Squares of Hanuman Dhoka (Kathmandu), Patan and Bhaktapur, the Buddhist stupas of Swayambhunath and Boudhanath and the Hindu temples of Pashupati and Changu Narayan.

23 ACAPULCO

The port of Acapulco is located in Guerrero state in southwestern Mexico. It is a popular resort city that has the best harbour on Mexico's Pacific coast and is one of the finest natural anchorages in the world.

Acapulco is famous for its explosive nightlife, postcard beaches, unlimited water sports, hotels, gourmet restaurants and the breath-taking physical beauty of the Acapulco Bay! It is also known for its pleasant climate.

24 CHOCOLATE HILLS

The Chocolate Hills are in Bohol, Philippines. There are 1776 hills spread across an area of approximately 50 square kilometres. Depending on the season, the Chocolate Hills change colour, varying from green to chocolate brown. Geologists believe that the hills were formed from marine limestone on top of a clay layer.

25 GREAT BARRIER REEF

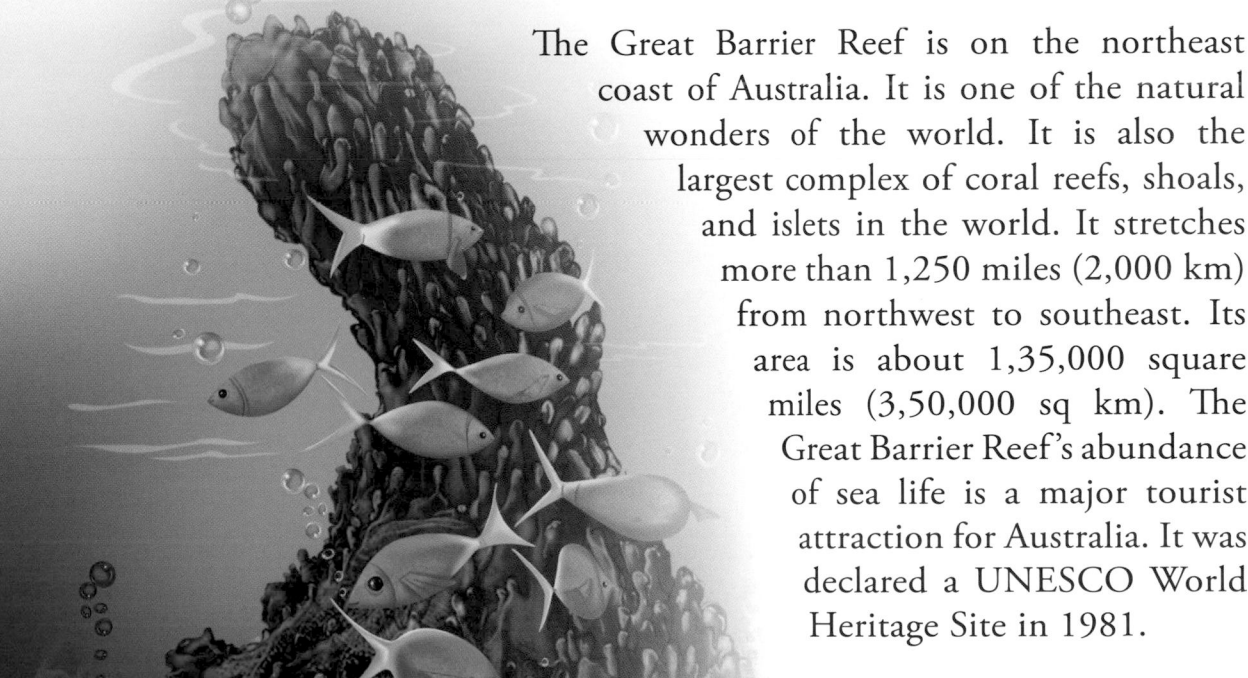

The Great Barrier Reef is on the northeast coast of Australia. It is one of the natural wonders of the world. It is also the largest complex of coral reefs, shoals, and islets in the world. It stretches more than 1,250 miles (2,000 km) from northwest to southeast. Its area is about 1,35,000 square miles (3,50,000 sq km). The Great Barrier Reef's abundance of sea life is a major tourist attraction for Australia. It was declared a UNESCO World Heritage Site in 1981.

26 VIENNA STATE OPERA

The local name of the Vienna State Opera is Staatsoper. It is a theatre in Vienna, Austria and one of the world's leading opera houses, known especially for performances of works by Richard Wagner, Wolfgang Amadeus Mozart and Richard Strauss.

27 AYERS ROCK

Ayers Rock is a giant monolith in Central Australia. It is called *Uluru* by the native people who consider it a sacred place. It is 3.6 kilometre long and rises almost 350 metres above the vast pancake-flat surrounding red sandy plain. The rock is most impressive at sunset, when it is coloured a fiery orange-red by the sun's rays.

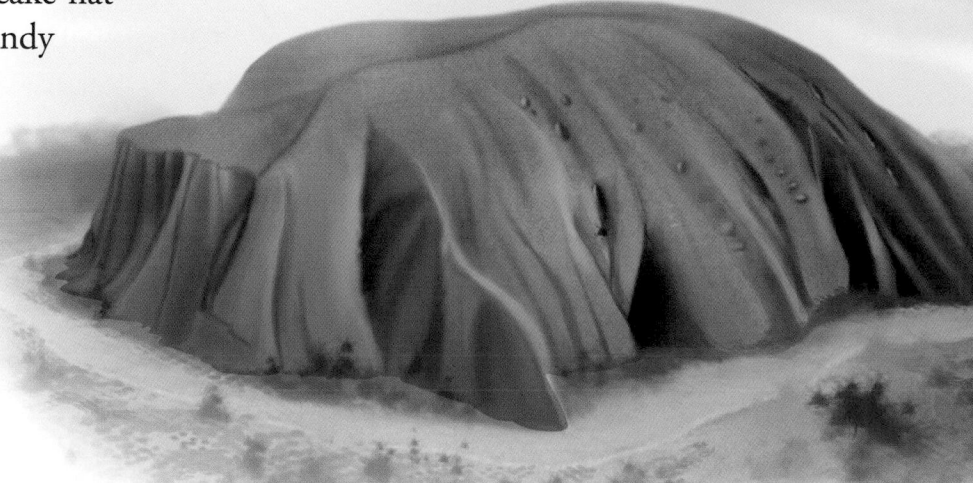

28 LOS GLACIARES NATIONAL PARK

Los Glaciares National Park is a World Heritage Site situated in southwest Santa Cruz province along the border with Chile. It has an area of 1722 square miles (4,459 sq km) and was established in 1937. The park is an area of dazzling natural beauty, with rough, towering mountains and numerous glacial lakes, including Lake Argentino, which is 160 kilometres long.

29 BANFF NATIONAL PARK

Banff National Park is in southwestern Alberta, Canada. It was established in 1885 as Canada's first national park. It covers an area of 6,641 square kilometres (2,564 miles). Banff was designated as part of the Canadian Rocky Mountain Parks World Heritage site in 1984. It contains active glaciers. A wide variety of animals like the grizzly and black bear, elk, moose, mule deer, wolf, caribou, mountain goat, marmot can be found here.

30 AJANTA CAVES

The Ajanta Caves are near the Ajanta village, Maharashtra, India. The first Buddhist cave monuments at Ajanta date from the 2nd and 1st centuries BC. There are approximately 30 caves at the site of Ajanta, of which cave numbers 9, 10, 19, 26 and 29 are *caityas* (sanctuaries) and the rest are *vihāras* (monasteries). The carvings and the paintings in the caves depict the life of Lord Buddha. Along with this, several types of human and animal figures are also carved out of the rocks. The caves have been designated as a UNESCO World Heritage Site.

31 VALLEY OF THE KINGS

The Valley of the Kings lies on the Nile's west bank near Luxor. During Egypt's New Kingdom (1539–1075 BC), the valley became a royal burial ground for pharaohs such as Tutankhamen, Seti I, and Ramses II, as well as for the queens, high priests and other elites of the 18th, 19th and 20th dynasties. In 1979, UNESCO designated the valley as part of the World Heritage Site of ancient Thebes. The Valley of the Kings has two components: the East Valley and the West Valley. It is the East Valley which most tourists visit and in which most of the tombs of the New Kingdom Pharaohs can be found.

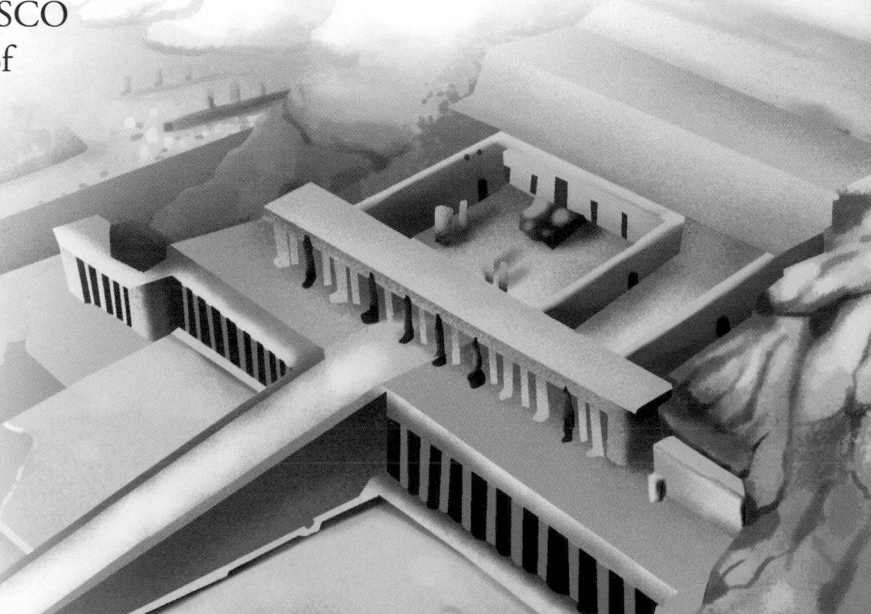

Did You Know?

- The amount of iron and steel used in the building of the Itaipu Dam would be enough to build 380 Eiffel Towers.
- The Sleeping Beauty Castle's design in Disneyland was inspired by the Neuschwanstein Castle.

1 GREAT WALL OF CHINA

The Great Wall of China is one of the largest building construction projects ever completed. It was built over 2,000 years ago by Qin Shihuangdi, the first emperor of China (221–206 BC). In Chinese, the wall is called '*Wan-Li Qang-Qeng*' which means 10,000 Li Long Wall (10,000 Li = about 5,000 km). It was made for defence against raids by the nomadic people. The longest wall in the world, it is an amazing feat of ancient defensive architecture.

It is one of the Seven Wonders of the World and was listed as a World Heritage Site by UNESCO in 1987. The wall winds up and down across deserts, grasslands, mountains and plateaus, stretching approximately 8,851.8 kilometres (5,500 miles) from the east to the west of China.

The wall is a simple structure. It is built of dirt, stone and brick. Its height ranges from 15 to 30 feet (5 to 9 m), with watchtowers rising at regular intervals above it. It is 15 to 25 feet (5 to 8 m) wide. Along the top runs a 13-foot (4 m) wide roadway. Behind the wall there are, at intervals, permanent camps for troops.

During its construction, the Great Wall was called 'the longest cemetery on Earth' because so many people died building it. Reportedly, it cost the lives of more than one million people.

With a history of more than 2,000 years, some of the sections are now in ruins or have disappeared. However, it is still one of the most alluring attractions all around the world owing to its architectural grandeur and historical significance.

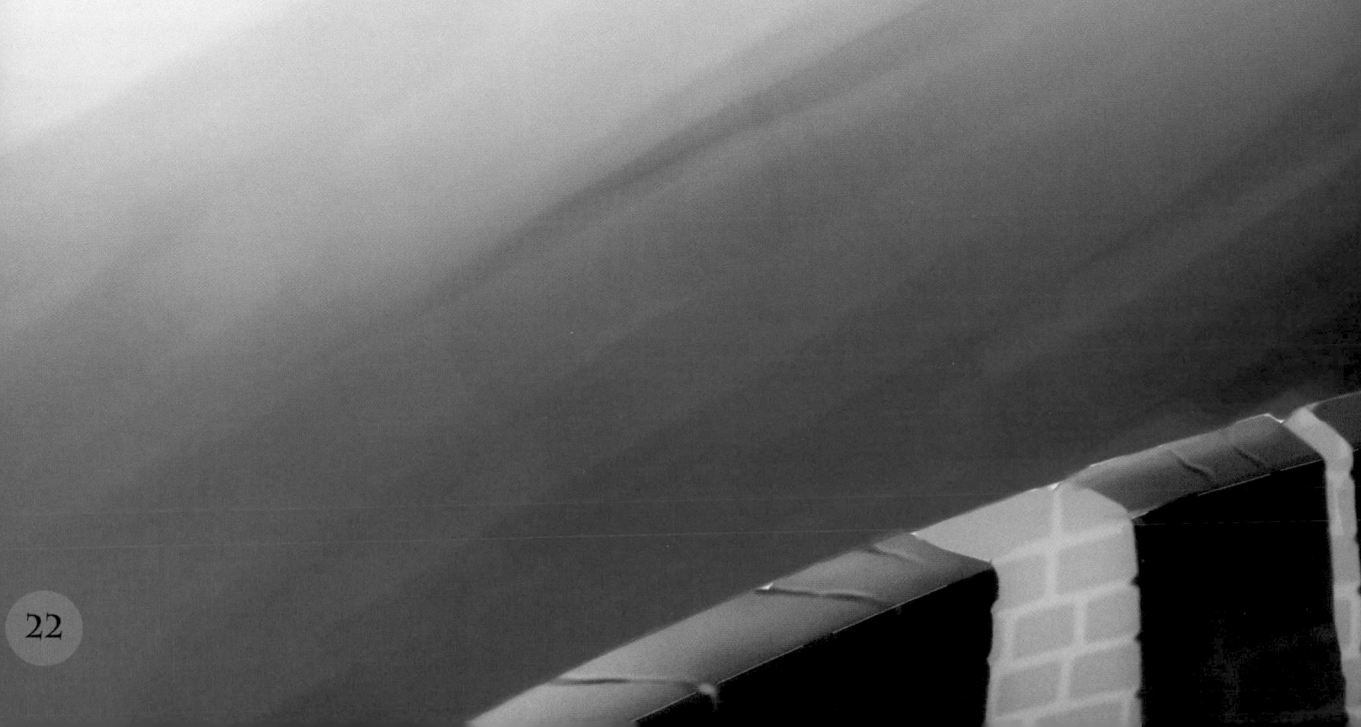

2 ITAIPU DAM

Itaipu Dam is located on the upper Paraná River at the Brazil-Paraguay border. It is one of the world's largest hydroelectric projects. It took 18 years to build at a cost of about US$ 18 billion.

Its 18 massive turbine generators, located in the powerhouse at the base of the dam, are capable of generating 12,600 megawatts of electricity. The dam is a major tourist attraction. More than nine million visitors from 162 countries have visited the structure since it was completed in 1991.

3 MINARET OF JAM

The Minaret of Jam is located in Afghanistan. It is 65 metres tall, dating back to the 12th century. It is covered in elaborate brickwork with a blue tile inscription at the top. The minaret is noteworthy for the quality of its architecture and decoration. The Minaret of Jam was the first site in Afghanistan to be placed in the UNESCO World Heritage list in 2002.

4 BAFFIN ISLAND

Baffin Island lies between Greenland and the Canadian mainland. With an area of 1,95,928 square miles (5,07,451 sq km), it is the largest island in Canada and the fifth largest in the world. Baffin Island offers visitors such unique experiences as viewing polar bears, the Northern Lights and kayaking between ice flows.

5 TERRACOTTA WARRIORS

The terracotta army is part of an elaborate mausoleum created to accompany the first emperor of China into the afterlife, according to archaeologists.

The terracotta warriors and horses were discovered accidentally when some local farmers sank a well at the foot of Mt. Lishan in 1974. Excavation was later carried on the site. They found not one, but thousands of clay soldiers, each with unique facial expressions and positioned according to their ranks. Further excavations revealed swords, arrow tips and other weapons, many in perfect conditions.

The Terracotta Warriors are the most significant archeological discovery of the 20th century in China. They are acclaimed to be on the same level of historical importance as the pyramids of Egypt and the sculptures of ancient Greece. The museum is a major world tourist destination.

6 JAISALMER FORT

The Jaisalmer Fort is in Jaisalmer, Rajasthan. The fort was built in 1156 and is the second oldest in the state of Rajasthan. It was built by Raja Jaisal from where it derives its name. The fort is 250 feet tall and reinforced by an imposing sandstone wall of 30 feet. The fort has 99 bastions. Its massive sandstone walls are a yellowish-brown in colour during the day, turning to a magical honey-gold as the sun sets camouflaging the fort and making it appear a part of the picturesque yellow desert. Thus, it is also known as the 'Golden Fort'.

7 CN TOWER

The Canadian National Tower, better known as CN Tower, is the world's tallest free-standing structure. It is located in Toronto, Canada. The tower was constructed by the Canadian National Railroad to improve television reception. The CN Tower attracts approximately 2 million visitors each year. Though the tower primarily functions for radio and television signals, it also has attractive features for visitors. At the top of the tower are a revolving CN Tower restaurant and lookout platforms.

8 BASILICA NOTRE DAME DE LA PAIX

Basilica Notre Dame de la Paix is located at Yamoussoukro, Ivory Coast. Basilica Notre Dame de la Paix is also known as Basilica of Our Lady of Peace of Yamoussoukro. It is considered the tallest and largest church in the world. It was constructed between 1985 and 1989 at a cost of $300 million. It is constructed entirely of marble (30 acres) imported from Italy and decorated with 23,000 square feet (7,000 sq m) of contemporary stained glass from France. Basilica Notre Dame de la Paix is designed after Rome's Basilica of Saint Peter. It can accommodate 18,000 people, a total of 7,000 seated and 11,000 standing.

9 KARNAK TEMPLE

The Karnak Temple is a vast temple complex in Luxor, Egypt. This complex was known as *Ipet-isut* (most select of places) by the ancient Egyptians. It is a city of temples built over 2,000 years. The Karnak complex is the work of several pharaohs and is dedicated to the supreme deity Amon-Ra. The site consists of several huge temples, columns, pylons and obelisks. It was listed as a World Heritage Site by UNESCO in 1998.

10 IGUAZU FALLS

Iguazu Falls are a series of waterfalls at the Argentina-Brazil border. The name '*Iguazu*' comes from the local Indian language and means 'big water'. The falls themselves actually consist of over 270 separate falls that stretch for more than one and a half miles. Most of the individual waterfalls are about 200 feet in height. The most famous of them all is known as The Devil's Throat. It is a U-shaped waterfall that is almost 500 feet across and over 2,000 feet in length. UNESCO designated the falls as a World Heritage Site in 1986. The falls are a popular tourist destination in South America.

11 BALI

Bali is in Indonesia. It is one of the most popular holiday spots in the world. Bali is also known as the Island of the Gods. Most of Bali is mountainous, the highest point being Mount Agung, or Bali Peak, 10,308 feet (3,142 m) high and locally known as the 'navel of the world.' The giant banyan (waringin) trees are held sacred by the Balinese.

12 AMAZON RAINFOREST

The Amazon Rainforest, also known as the Amazon Jungle, is located in South America and covers the Amazon River basin. This rainforest is the largest rainforest in the world. The Amazon Rainforest contains several insects, plants, birds, and other forms of life. A wide variety of trees can be found, including many species of myrtle, laurel, palm, and acacia, as well as rosewood, Brazil nut, and rubber tree. Its wildlife includes jaguar, manatee, tapir, red deer, capybara and many other types of rodents, and several types of monkeys.

13 NGORONGORO CRATER

The Ngorongoro Crater is in Tanzania. It is a deep volcanic crater and is almost 3 million years old. It is also known as 'Africa's Garden of Eden.' The crater is home to over 30,000 animals including elephants, lions, cheetahs, wildebeests, buffaloes and the rare black rhinos. UNESCO designated the caldera as a World Heritage Site in 1979.

14 BAGAN

Bagan is in Myanmar. It is also known as Pagan. Bagan is a pilgrimage centre and contains ancient Buddhist shrines that have been restored and are currently in use. This region was the capital of the ancient kings of Bagan. It was probably built in AD 849. The golden Shwezigon Paya is one of its most significant religious buildings. There are over 2,000 pagodas and temples in Bagan.

15 TEOTIHUACÁN

Teotihuacán is located in Mexico. The name 'Teotihuacán' means 'The City of the Gods' or 'Where Men Become Gods' (in Nahuatl). Teotihuacán was designated a UNESCO World Heritage Site in 1987. The ancient city of Teotihuacán is the most visited of Mexico's archaeological sites. It was built between the 1st and 7th centuries. Some of its famous monuments are the Temple of Quetzalcoatl and the Pyramids of the Sun and the Moon.

16 BORA BORA

Bora Bora is an island in the Leeward group of the Society Islands of French Polynesia. It is volcanic in origin. The island is about 6 miles (10 km) long and 2.5 miles (4 km) wide. It is surrounded by coral reefs. The original name of the island in the Tahitian language is Porapora meaning 'First Born'.

17 POTALA PALACE

Potala Palace is in Lhasa, Tibet. It is the winter palace of the Dalai Lama and is at an altitude of 3,700 m. The palace complex comprises the White and Red Palaces. It has a huge collection of materials and articles of Tibetan history, religion, culture and art. In 1994, the Potala Palace was designated a UNESCO World Heritage Site.

18 NEUSCHWANSTEIN CASTLE

The Neuschwanstein Castle is located in Bavaria, Germany. It was built by King Ludwig II of Bavaria, also known as the 'Fairytale King.' Neuschwanstein literally means '*New Swan Castle*.' Its construction was begun in 1869 and left unfinished after King Louis's death in 1886. The look of the Neuschwanstein castle motivated Walt Disney to create the Magic Kingdom. It is the most visited castle in Germany.

19 HERMITAGE MUSEUM

The Hermitage Museum is located in St. Petersburg. It was founded in 1764. It is one of the largest and oldest museums of the world. The museum has about 2.7 million exhibits. It includes works by Leonardo da Vinci, Michelangelo, Raphael, Titian, Rembrandt and others. The main architectural collection of the Hermitage consists of the Winter Palace, the former state residence of the Russian emperors, the buildings of the Small, Old (Great) and New Hermitages, the Hermitage Theatre and the Auxiliary House.

20 ABBEY OF ST. GALL

The Abbey of St. Gall is situated in the city of St. Gallen, Switzerland. It was founded by St. Othmar in the 8th century. On the site of what is now the cathedral, Gallus, an Irish monk, had once erected his hermitage. He attracted many fellow-believers and soon became a well-known preacher in Switzerland.

The library of the Abbey of St. Gall is one of the richest and oldest in the world, containing precious manuscripts which include the Plan of Saint Gall—the only surviving major architectural drawing from the Early Middle Ages. It became a part of the UNESCO World Heritage Site list in 1983.

21 ANGEL FALLS

The Angel Falls is located in Venezuela. It is the highest waterfall in the world with a drop of 3,212 feet. The falls was discovered by James C. Angel in 1935. Angel Falls is also called *Kerepakupai meru* which means 'Waterfall of the Deepest Place.'

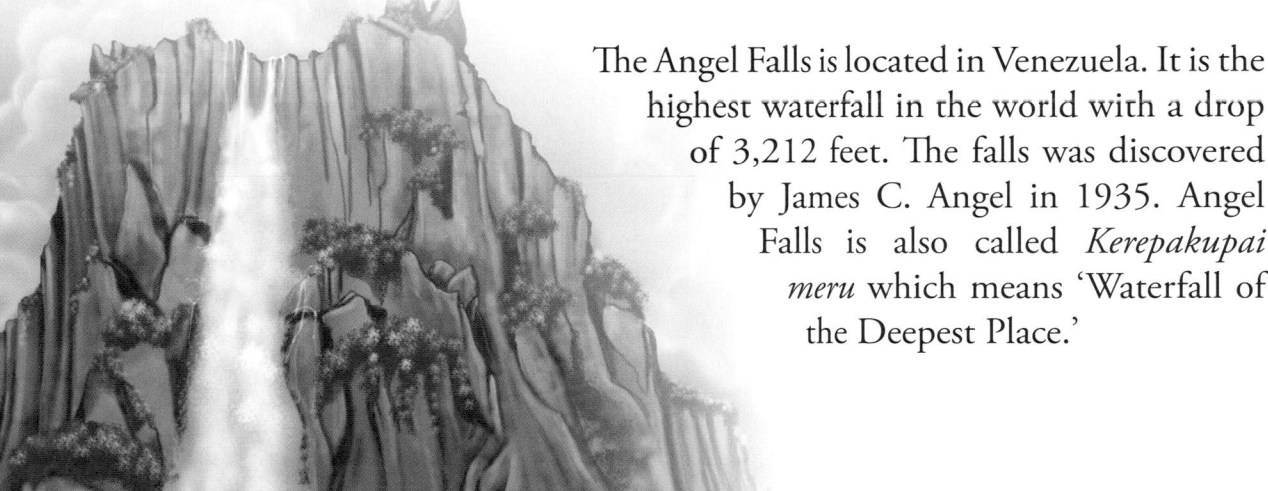

22 TOPKAPI PALACE MUSEUM

The Topkapi Palace is in Istanbul. It is the oldest and the largest of the remaining palaces in the world. It was converted into a museum in 1924. There are 18,000 manuscripts, more than 23,000 archival documents, and private papers of different sultans. It also contains a selection of Islamic relics. It is one of Istanbul's most popular sights.

23 BAALBEK

Baalbek is the name of an archeological site in Lebanon. In Roman times, it was known as Heliopolis or City of the Sun. The complex was designated a UNESCO World Heritage Site in 1984. Baalbek has breathtaking temples and city ruins which are among the leading and finest examples of Roman architecture in the world. One of the main structures on the site is the Temple of Jupiter, of which only portions remain. The Temple of Bacchus and the Temple of Venus are the other important structures.

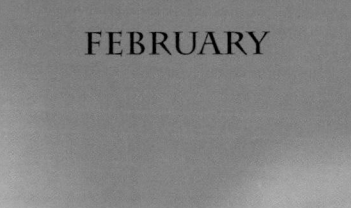

24 SAHARA DESERT

The Sahara Desert, which covers most of North Africa, is the largest desert in the world. It covers an area of approximately 3.5 million square miles. On the west, the Sahara is surrounded by the Atlantic Ocean and on the east by the Red Sea, and to the north are the Atlas Mountains and the Mediterranean Sea. The name 'Sahara' comes from the Arabic noun 'sahra', meaning desert, and its plural, 'sahara'.

The sand dunes of the dessert are very big, so huge that they can go up to a height of 600 feet. Additionally, there are stone plateaus, salt flats, gravel plains and arid valleys. Sandstorms are very common in the desert.

The highest part of the desert is at the summit of Mount Koussi, which is 11,204 feet (3,415 m) high. The lowest point of the Sahara is 436 feet (133 m) below sea level in the Qattera Depression in Egypt.

The plant life is thin with scattered concentrations of grasses and shrubs. There are many animals in the desert, including poisonous snakes and poisonous spiders, scorpions, monitor lizards, sand vipers, wild dogs, ostriches, cheetahs, among others.

25 SHWEDAGON PAGODA

The Shwedagon Pagoda is in Myanmar. It is also known as the Shwedagon Paya. The Pagoda is 321.5 feet high. Its top is made up of gold and has lots of diamonds, rubies and precious gems set in it. It is a stunning work of Burmese temple architecture and is the holiest Buddhist shrine in Myanmar.

The legend of the Schwedagon Pagoda begins with two Burmese merchant brothers who met the Buddha himself. The Buddha gave them eight of his hairs to be enshrined in Burma. With the help of spirits and the king of the region, the brothers discovered the hill where the relics of the previous Buddhas had been enshrined. This is where the pagoda was built.

26 VARANASI

Varanasi, also known as Benares, Banaras, Kashi or Kasi, is on the banks of the Ganges River in Uttar Pradesh. It is the world's oldest living city. The city is considered the most sacred place for Hindus.

The name 'Varanasi' is derived from the twin tributaries of Ganga, namely, Varuna and Asi. Varanasi is chiefly known to travellers for its *ghats* (stone steps leading directly into the water).

The city is also a centre of arts and crafts and of music and dance. Varanasi is famous for silk weaving and its silk saris with gold and silver threadwork, as well as for wooden toys, bangles made of glass, ivory work and its brassware.

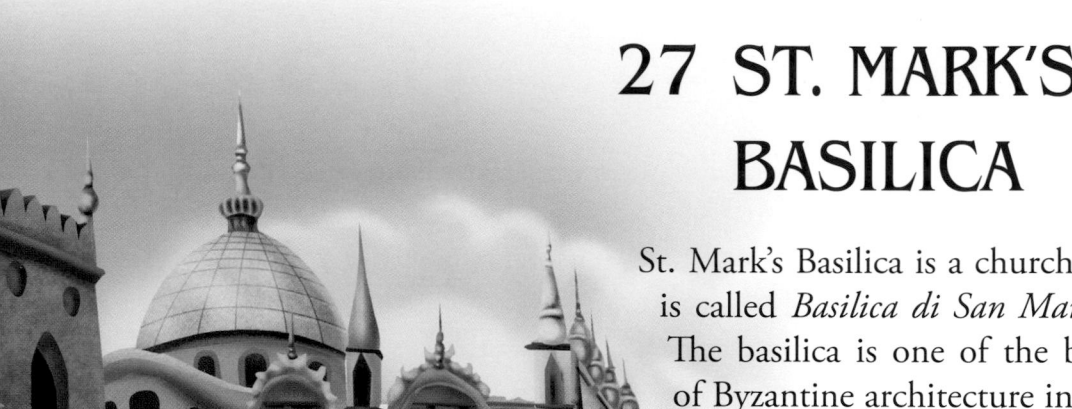

27 ST. MARK'S BASILICA

St. Mark's Basilica is a church in Venice. It is called *Basilica di San Marco* in Italian. The basilica is one of the best examples of Byzantine architecture in the world. It has been the seat of the Archbishop of Venice since 1807.

The interior is decorated throughout with mosaics on gold ground and with many varieties of marble.

28 DELPHI

Delphi is one of the most important archaeological sites of Greece. It was designated a UNESCO World Heritage Site in 1987. Delphi was the seat of the Oracle. Since the Oracle could predict the future, most of the kings and common people used to consult the Oracle on matters that were of great importance. Some sites to visit in Delphi are the famous Temple of Apollo, the Tholos, the Delphi Museum and the Charioteer of Delphi.

Did You Know?

- There are more than 350 clocks and watches—one of the largest collections of working clocks in the world—in Buckingham palace.
- The figure of Goddess Meenakshi in Meenakshi Temple is said to be carved out of a solo emerald.

1 GRAND CANYON

Carved out by the Colorado River, the Grand Canyon (nearly 1500 m deep) is the most spectacular gorge in the world and is located in the state of Arizona, U.S. It is 277 mile (446 km) long.

It is noted for its fantastic shapes and colours. The colour of the canyon is red, but each layer has a unique shade—green and pink, buff and gray and brown, slate-gray and violet.

It is home to approximately 70 species of mammals, 250 species of birds, 25 types of reptiles and five species of amphibians. Willow trees and cotton-woods grow there too.

The Grand Canyon, with its mile-high, multicoloured rock walls, craggy cliffs, and sandy slopes, is the embodiment of nature's awesome power and unsurpassable beauty.

2 GOLDEN PAVILION

The Golden Pavilion is located in Kyoto, Japan. It is also called *Kinkaku-ji* in Japanese. It was built in 1397. The building was originally constructed for shogun Ashikaga Yoshimitsu in 1397 as a retirement home and became a Zen temple upon his death. People visit its grounds to enjoy its peaceful surroundings and architecture.

3 MEENAKSHI TEMPLE

Meenakshi Temple is situated in Madurai, Tamil Nadu, India. It is a fine example of the Dravidian architecture. This temple complex is devoted to Shiva, known here as Sundareshvara and his wife Parvati or Meenakshi.

The whole temple complex is surrounded by 12 *gopurams* (towers), among which the southern tower rises to more than 170 feet high. The image of Goddess Meenakshi is said to be carved out of a single emerald. This beautiful temple was renovated by various kings over time.

4 POMPEII

Pompeii is the ancient city of Campania, Italy. It was buried by a volcanic eruption of Mount Vesuvius in AD 79. About 2000 years later, archaeologists uncovered the city. Pompeii, Herculaneum and Torre Annunziata were jointly declared a World Heritage Site by UNESCO in 1997.

5 HAGIA SOPHIA

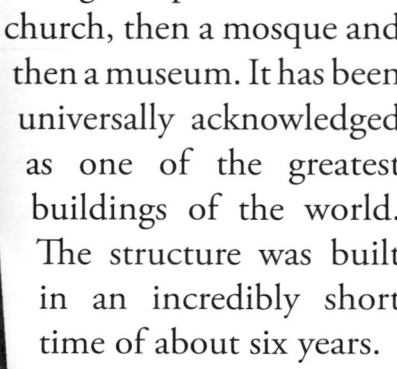

Hagia Sophia is in Istanbul. It is also called the Church of the Holy Wisdom. The Hagia Sophia was first a church, then a mosque and then a museum. It has been universally acknowledged as one of the greatest buildings of the world. The structure was built in an incredibly short time of about six years.

6 MECCA

Mecca (*Makkah*) is in Saudi Arabia. Prophet Muhammad, the founder of Islam, was born in Mecca. The Prophet himself chose Mecca as the holy city of Islam. Each year, during the Islamic month of *Dhu'l-Hijja*, thousands of Muslims from around the world join in a pilgrimage (*Haj*) to Mecca.

7 MOUNT EVEREST

The Everest lies in the Himalayan mountain range along the border of Nepal and Tibet. It is the highest mountain in the world at a height of 29,035 feet (8850 m). Its Tibetan name is *Chomolungma* meaning 'Goddess Mother of the World' or 'Goddess of the Valley.' In Sanskrit it is known as *Sagarmatha* meaning 'Ocean Mother.' Mount Everest is named after Sir George Everest, who was the British Surveyor-General of India from 1830 to 1843. Sir Edmund Hillary and Sherpa Tenzing Norgay became the first men known to have reached the Everest's summit in 1953.

The Everest has a temperature of about -33° Fahrenheit (-36° Celcius) and can drop as low as -76° Fahrenheit (-60° Celcius). Many men and women have risked their lives to climb the mountain.

8 DAMASCUS

Damascus is the capital of Syria and one of the most ancient cities in the world. It has been called the 'Pearl of the East.' It was founded in the 3rd millennium BC. During the Middle Ages, it was the centre of a prosperous craft industry, specialising in swords and lace. There are about 125 monuments from different periods of its history. The most impressive is the 8th-century Great Mosque of the Umayyads. The Old City was designated a UNESCO World Heritage Site in 1979.

9 CARLSBAD CAVERNS NATIONAL PARK

Carlsbad Caverns National Park is in New Mexico. The park was first designated a National Monument in 1923. It was redesignated a National Park in 1930. Finally, it was designated a UNESCO World Heritage Site in 1995. The most well-known part of this National Park are the Carlsbad Caverns. This park was established to preserve Carlsbad Caverns and numerous other caves. The park has 83 separate caves, including the nation's deepest and third-longest limestone cave.

10 BANAUE RICE TERRACES

The Banaue Rice Terraces are in the Philippines. They are the most-visited tourist attractions of the Philippines. The terraces were carved from the hillside by the Ifugao tribes people about 2000 years ago. The tribal people did not use any machinery to level the steps. The Banaue Rice Terraces were declared a World Heritage Site by UNESCO in 1995.

11 ACROPOLIS

The Acropolis is in Athens, Greece. The word Acropolis (*akro + polis*) literally means edge or point of the city. Visitors from all over the world come to see the Acropolis. The three important temples here are the Parthenon, the Erechteion and the Temple of Nike. The Parthenon is the major attraction of the Acropolis complex. It was designated a World Heritage Site in 1987.

12 JERUSALEM OLD CITY

Jerusalem Old City is in Israel. It is a sacred city for the Muslims, Jews and Christians: for the Muslims because it is the site of the Temple Mount where the Prophet Muhammad rose to heaven; for the Jews because it is the home of the Wailing Wall (remains of the Second Temple); and finally for the Christians because it is where Christ was crucified.

There are about 220 historic monuments in the city. In 1982, the city was designated a UNESCO World Heritage Site.

13 CAPPADOCIA

Cappadocia is in Central Turkey. It is well known for its exceptional geological features called fairy chimneys. These large, cone-like formations were created over time by erosion of the soft volcanic ash around them. There are many places to be seen in Cappadocia like the Fairy Chimneys, Göreme Valley National Park and rock churches, underground cities of Kaymakli, Derinkuyu or Ozkonak, Zelve Valley and Pasabag, Avanos with its pottery and carpets, Uçhisar rock fortress, Ortahisar rock fortress, Ürgüp, Ihlara valley, Soganli, Sinasos and Hacibektas.

14 FJORDS OF NORWAY

The Fjords of Norway were carved from the mountains along the coastline by slow-moving glaciers. The Fjords offer a magnificent view of steep cliffs, lush green slopes, and snow-capped mountains. In 2000, along the bottoms of the Norwegian Fjords, a few of the world's largest coral reefs were discovered.

One of the most famous Fjord in Norway is called the Sognafjord, the King of Fjord. It is 1200 metres deep and 200 kilometres long.

15 ST. PETER'S BASILICA

St. Peter's Basilica is in Rome. Its construction was begun by Pope Julius II in 1506. It was completed in 1615 under Paul V. The church is a major pilgrimage site. The interior of the church is filled with many masterpieces of Renaissance and Baroque art. The most famous are Michelangelo's Pietà, the Baldachin by Bernini over the main altar, the statue of St. Longinus in the crossing, the tomb of Urban VIII and the bronze cathedral of St. Peter in the apse. Until 1989, St. Peter's was the largest church in Christendom.

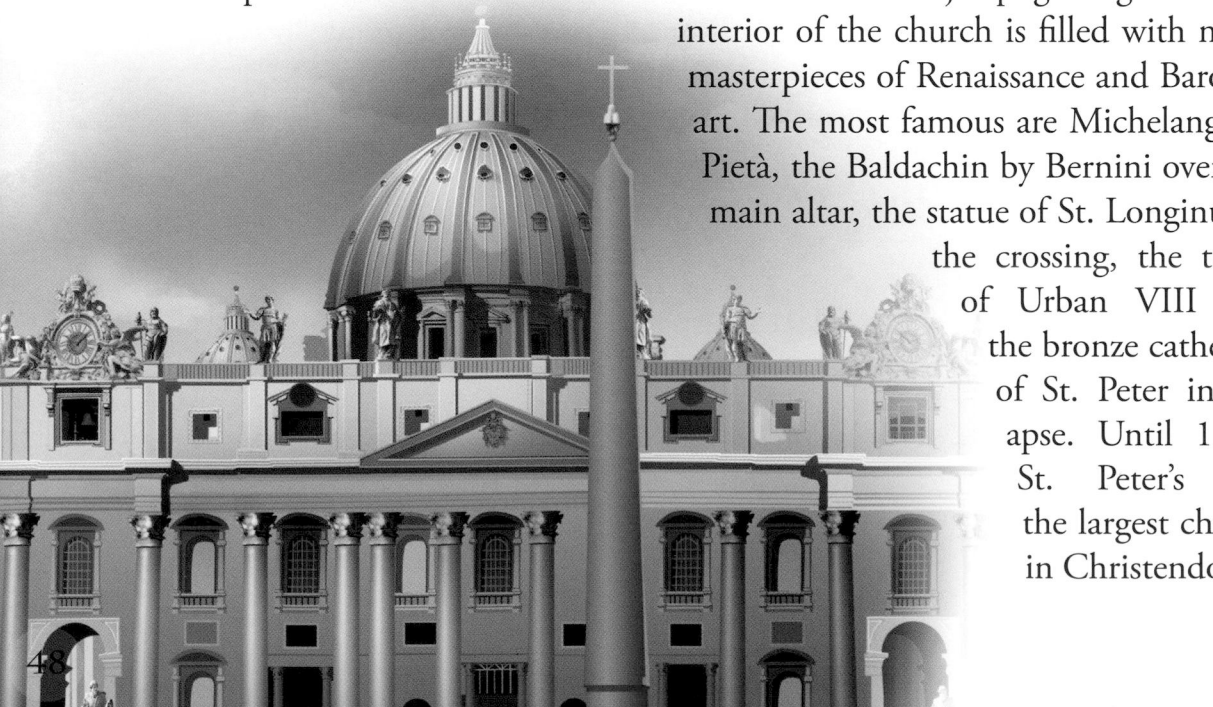

16 EGYPTIAN MUSEUM

Also known as the Egyptian Antiquities Museum, the Egyptian Museum is located in Cairo. It holds the largest collection of Ancient Egyptian artifacts in the world. The Museum was founded in the 19th century by French Egyptologist Auguste Mariette. There are more than 100,000 items in the museum. Some of the items are the gold mask that covered Tutankhamen's head, reliefs, jewellery, ornaments of all kinds, among other objects. There is a black granite sculpture of Queen Nefertiti. There are also two granite figures of Queen Hatshepsut and colossal figures of Amenhotep IV from Karnak.

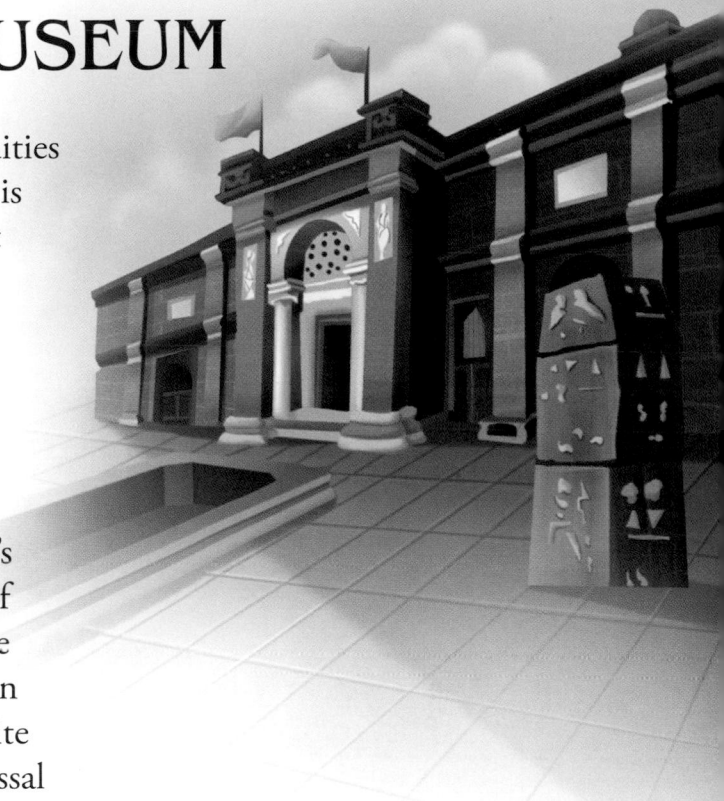

17 BOROBUDUR

Borobudur is in Java, Indonesia. The name Borobudur means 'many Buddhas.' It is the temple of one of the greatest Buddhist monuments in the world. The monument has 1500 panels carved in relief with scenes of the Buddha's life. This temple was built by the Sailendra dynasty between AD 778 and 842. It was designated a UNESCO World Heritage Site in 1991. The Borobudur monument combines the symbolic forms of the stupa, the temple mountain and the mandala. The site was abandoned 200 years later and was rediscovered by an English army officer in the 19th century.

18 HONG KONG HARBOUR

The Hong Kong Harbour is located between the Hong Kong Island and Kowloon Peninsula. It is also known as Victoria Harbour. During the second night of the lunar year, there is a fantastic display of fireworks one can witness. Hence, it is popular with tourists. It is one of the world's busiest natural harbours. Hong Kong's striking coastline around the harbour creates an exciting view. Cruises set sail from piers on either side of Victoria Harbour. Among the best places to view the Harbour is the Victoria Tower on the Victoria Peak, or from a piazza at the Culture Centre. Rides on the Star Ferry to view the harbour are also very popular among tourists.

19 SISTINE CHAPEL

The Sistine Chapel is in the Vatican City. The chapel was commissioned by Pope Sixtus IV in 1475. It was designed to be the Pope's chapel and the site of papal elections. The architect was Giovanni dei Dolci. The frescoes on the ceiling, collectively known as the Sistine Ceiling, were commissioned by Pope Julius II in 1508 and were painted by Michelangelo. They depict incidents from the Old Testament. The Sistine Chapel is a rectangular brick building with six arched windows on each of the two main (or side) walls and a barrel-vaulted ceiling.

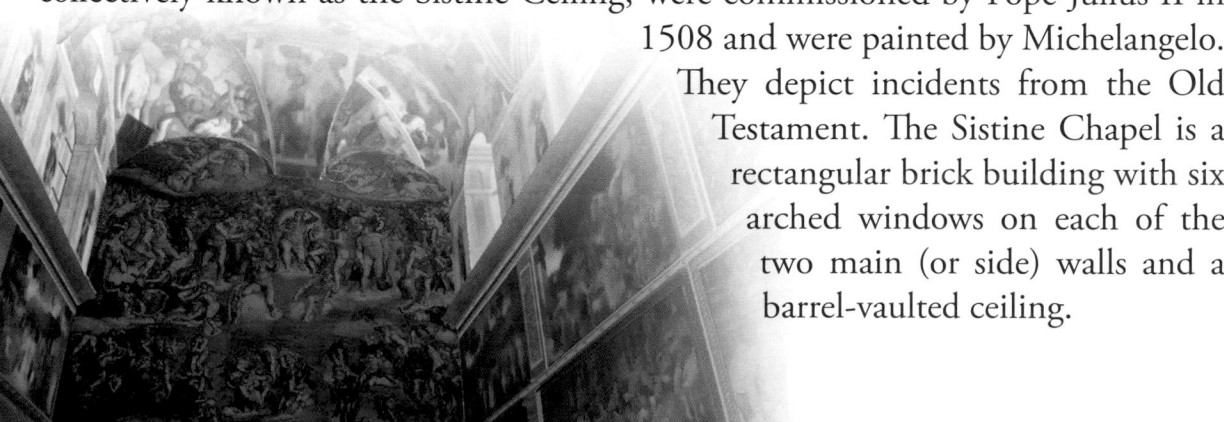

20 BURJ KHALIFA

The Burj Khalifa is a skyscraper in Dubai. It rises 2717 feet (828 m) into the sky. It is the tallest building in the world. The skyscraper has 162 floors. An observation on the 124th floor allows a 360° view of the city. Its construction began in 2004. The costs exceeded $20 billion, and nearly 12,000 people worked on it. The Burj Khalifa has the highest mosque (158th floor) and the highest swimming pool (76th floor) in the world. Fireworks and celebrations highlighted the official opening of the building in 2010.

21 ALHAMBRA

Alhambra is in Granada, Spain. The name 'Alhambra' in Arabic means 'red,' and is probably derived from the colour of the sun-dried bricks of which the outer walls are built. The palace was built chiefly between 1238 and 1358, during the reign of Ibn al-Ahmar.

The structure, which covers an area of 13 hectares, is renowned for its stunning frescoes and interior detail. The building is one of the finest examples of Moorish architecture in the world and is among Europe's most-visited tourist attractions.

Alhambra was designated a UNESCO World Heritage Site in 1984.

22 LOUVRE MUSEUM

The Louvre Museum is in Paris. It is called *Musée du Louvre* in French. In 1527, King Francis I razed the original building and started construction on what we know as the Louvre Museum.

Beginning with the reign of Charles V, the Louvre became a place to store works of art. It contained Charles V's private collection of books and artworks. Subsequent monarchs kept adding to the collection.

Today, the grand museum contains more than 300,000 works of art. There are paintings by Leonardo da Vinci, like the *Mona Lisa,* and also works of Raphael. Also on display are famous sculptures, like the *Venus de Milo* and the *Winged Victory of Samothrace.*

23 BUCKINGHAM PALACE

The Buckingham Palace is in Westminster, England. The palace is the official London residence of the British monarchs. It takes its name from the house built for John Sheffield, Duke of Buckingham. In 1762, George III bought it for his wife, Queen Charlotte, and it became to be known as the queen's house. John Nash converted the house into a palace in the 1820s.

The palace has 775 rooms. These include 19 state rooms, 52 royal and guest bedrooms, 188 staff bedrooms, 92 offices and 78 bathrooms. The palace is 108 metres long across the front, 120 metres deep and 24 metres high. The total floor area of the palace, from basement to the roof covers over 77,000 square metres. The garden covers 40 acres, and includes a helicopter landing area, a lake, and a tennis court. It is home to 30 different species of birds and more than 350 different wild flowers, some of them extremely rare.

24 DEVILS TOWER NATIONAL MONUMENT

The Devils Tower National Monument is in Wyoming, U.S. It was the first American national monument and was established in 1906. It is also known as Bears Lodge. President Theodore Roosevelt proclaimed Devils Tower as the first national monument in 1906. The Devils Tower rises 1267 feet above the Belle Fourche River. It features a natural rock tower, the remnant of a volcanic interruption now exposed by erosion. This 1347-acre park is covered with pine forests, woodlands, and grasslands. Wild animals like the deer and prairie dog can be found here.

25 CHARLES BRIDGE

The Charles Bridge is built over River Vltava in Prague. It was commissioned by King Charles IV in 1357. The bridge spans the river with 16 pillars. It is the oldest bridge in the city. It is lined with statues and lamps. Charles Bridge is one of the most important tourist attractions in the city. The bridge was originally called the Stone Bridge or the Prague Bridge but has been named the 'Charles Bridge' since 1870. The bridge was built by Petr Parléř. It was damaged by flood several times: in 1432, when the water demolished 5 pillars, in 1784 and 1890, when 2 pillars and 3 arches were demolished. It is said that egg yolks were mixed into the mortar to strengthen the construction of the bridge.

26 BEAUBOURG

Beaubourg is the popular name for the Georges Pompidou National Center for Art and Culture. It is located in Paris, France. It was named after the French president Georges Pompidou who commissioned it in 1969. It was designed by architects Renzo Piano of Italy and Richard Rogers of England along with a Danish engineering firm. It was opened in 1977. The Beaubourg is a famous tourist attraction. The six-story building has a major museum of modern and contemporary art, a public library, a cinema and performance halls.

27 STATUE OF ZEUS

The Statue of Zeus is at Olympia, Greece. It was considered one of the Seven Wonders of the Ancient World. This statue was commissioned around 438 BC by the Council of Olympia.

The statue was built by the Greek sculptor Phidias. It was placed in the huge Temple of Zeus at Olympia. The statue was almost 12 metres (40 ft) high. Zeus was seated on a magnificent throne of cedar wood, inlaid with ivory, gold, ebony and precious stones. In Zeus' right hand was a small statue of Nike, the Goddess of Victory, and in his left hand, a shining sceptre on which an eagle rested. The temple was destroyed in AD 426.

28 LEANING TOWER OF PISA

The Leaning Tower of Pisa is in Pisa, Italy. Its Italian name is *Torre Pendente di Pisa*. The tower is famous for the shifting of its sandy foundations that had led to a significant lean of 5.5 degrees. The construction of the tower began in 1173. Bonnano Pisano was its engineer. In 1990, the tower was closed and the bells silenced as engineers undertook a major straightening project. The tower is 8 stories high. The shape of the tower is cylindrical and to reach the top of the tower, you need to climb the 294 steps spiralling from the inner side of the tower walls. The height of the tower is 58.36 metres from the foundation and 55 metres from the ground.

29 LA SCALA

La Scala is one of the world's greatest opera houses. It is located in Milan, Italy. The opera house opened in 1778. It was designed by Giuseppe Piermarini. The opera house opened with a production of Antonio Salieri's *Europa Riconosciuta*. The building was remodelled in 1867, restored in 1946 after having been bombed in World War II, and renovated in 2002–2004. La Scala has been the scene of many famous opera premieres, among them are Bellini's *Norma*, Verdi's Otello and *Falstaff*, and Puccini's *Madama Butterfly* and *Turandot*.

30 AKASHI KAIKYO BRIDGE

Akashi Kaikyo Bridge, also called 'Pearl Bridge', is located in Japan. The bridge is the longest suspension bridge in the world with a length of 3911 metres (12,831 ft). It is probably Japan's greatest engineering feat. The construction was finished in a span of 12 years. It was completed in the year 1998. The bridge is designed in such a manner that the earthquakes and harsh sea currents do not damage it. It took two million workers to construct the bridge. About 1,81,000 tonnes of steel and 1.4 million cubic metres of concrete were used in its construction. The Akashi Kaiko Bridge acts as a link between the city of Kobe and Iwaya by crossing the Akashi strait.

31 TIMBUKTU

Timbuktu, also spelled Tombouctou, is a city in Mali. It is historically important as a post on the trans-Saharan caravan route. Timbuktu was a centre for the expansion of Islam (1400–1600). It is home of the prestigious Koranic Sankore University and other *madrasas*. Timbuktu was founded around AD 1100 as a seasonal camp by Tuareg nomads. The city was designated a UNESCO World Heritage Site in 1988. In the 14th century, Timbuktu became an important focal point of the gold-salt trade.

Its three great mosques, Djingareyber, Sankore and Sidi Yahia, recall Timbuktu's golden age. Although continuously restored, these monuments are today under threat from desertification.

Did You Know?

- It is said that the word 'bankruptcy' came from Ponte Vecchio. When a merchant failed to pay his debt, the table (*banco*) he used to sell his wares was broken (*rotto*) by soldiers. Not having a table anymore (*bancorotto*), meant the seller was bankrupt.

1 MACHU PICCHU

Machu Picchu was designated a UNESCO World Heritage Site in 1983. It is also one of the new Seven Wonders of the World. It is 7000 feet above the sea level and is nestled on a small hilltop between the Andean Mountain Range. It is the site of ancient Inca ruins. It is believed that the initial residents of Machu Picchu died within 100 years of its establishment due to small pox. It was then captured by the Spaniards and destroyed later. It is often referred to as 'The Lost City of the Incas'.

It was discovered in 1911 by Hiram Bingham, a Yale University professor. Its primary buildings are the Intihuatana, the Temple of the Sun, and the Room of the Three Windows. No one knows what the real purpose of Machu Picchu was. Some people contemplate it was a prison and some say it was a defensive retreat, but the most common belief is that Machu Picchu was the estate of an Inca emperor.

The high level of preservation and the general layout of the ruin are remarkable.

Machu Picchu is the most economically important tourist attraction in Peru, bringing in visitors from around the world.

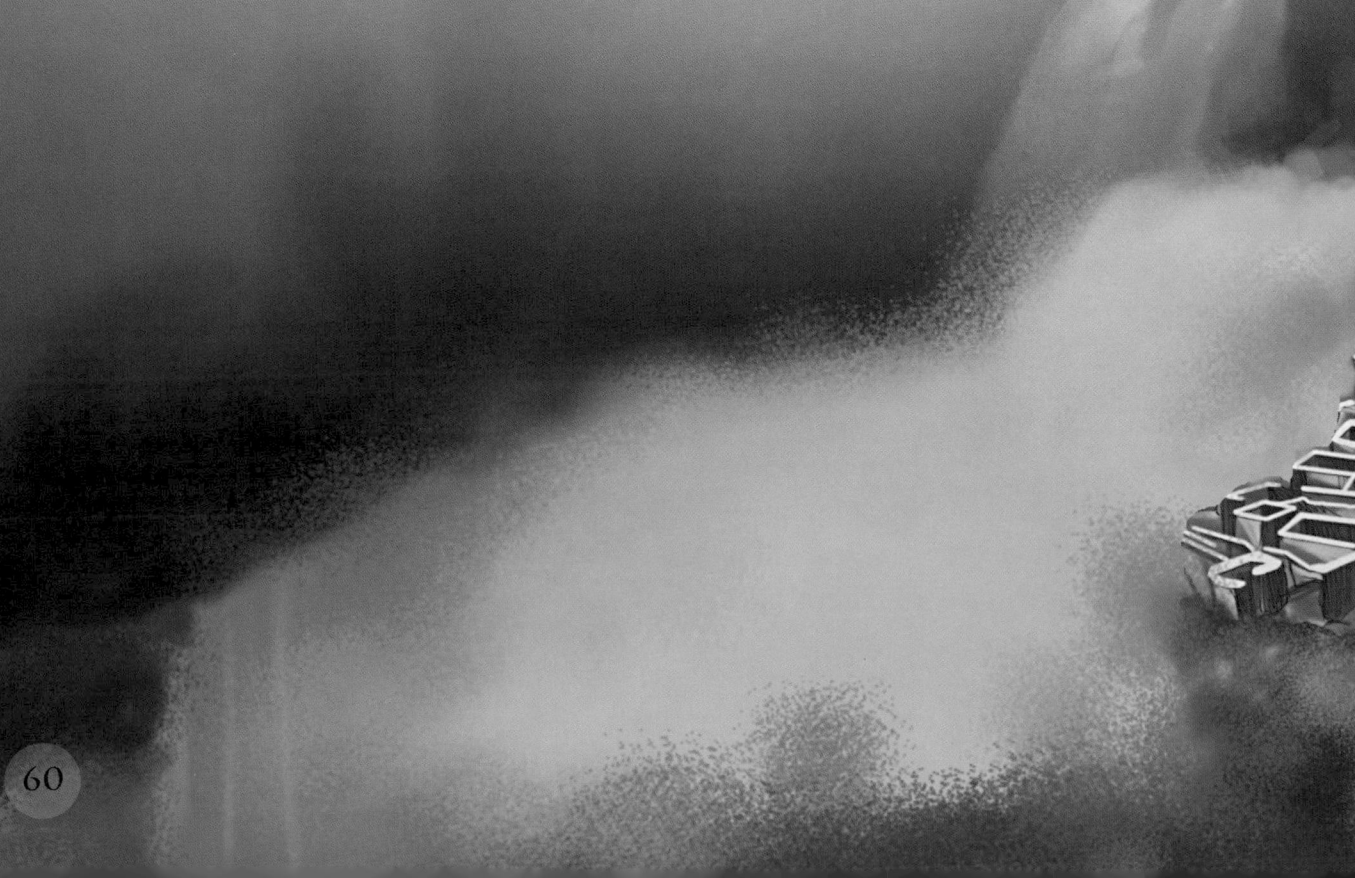

2 ELLORA CAVES

The caves are an impressive complex of Buddhist, Hindu and Jain temples near the ancient Indian village of Ellora, India. The UNESCO designated Ellora a World Heritage Site in 1983.

There are 34 caves in all: 12 Buddhist caves (200 BC to AD 600), 17 Hindu caves (AD 500 to 900) and 5 Jain caves (AD 800 to 1000). The Hindu caves are the most spectacular in design and the Buddhist caves contain the simplest decoration.

The most extraordinary of the cave temples is Kailasa (cave 16). This temple complex was carved downward and is therefore largely exposed to sunlight unlike the other caves which were carved horizontally into the rock face. It contains elaborately carved structures and halls with stairs, doorways, windows and numerous sculptures. Other decorations include a representation of the Hindu god Vishnu transformed into a man-lion and battling with a demon.

3 LORD HOWE ISLAND

Lord Howe Island is an island dependency of New South Wales, Australia. It is regarded as the most beautiful island in the Pacific and is volcanic in origin. The island was discovered in 1788. It is crescent-shaped with two peaks, Mounts Gower and Lidgbird, each rising above 2500 feet (760 m) at its southern end. Lord Howe Island group had been designated a UNESCO World Heritage Site for its rare collection of plants, birds, marine life and for its incredible beauty and scenery in 1982. The main income of the island is derived from tourism. The area of the island is 7 square miles (17 sq km).

4 LUNENBURG

Lunenburg is in Nova Scotia, Canada. This delightful place had its first settlements in 1753. It has retained its original layout and overall appearance, based on a rectangular grid pattern drawn up in the home country. Old town Lunenburg was designated a UNESCO World Heritage Site in 1995. The town of Lunenburg offers visitors many architectural delights. Apart from fishing and fish processing, economic activities focus on shipbuilding and market gardening. The Nova Scotia Fisheries Exhibition and Fishermen's Reunion is held at Lunenburg each September. Historic buildings include St. John's Anglican Church (1754) and Zion Evangelical Lutheran Church (1776).

5 BAISHUI TERRACE

Baishui Terrace is located in Zhongdian, China. The terrace is also known as the White Water Terrace. It is also regarded as the crib of the Naxi culture. The Baishui Terrace was formed by the gathering of calcium carbonate deposits left behind by flowing spring water. The terrace slope is 140 metres long and 160 metres wide and has a semicircular platform pool on the top that is surrounded by white limestone. According to legend, the first saint of the Dongba religion was attracted by the fascinating scenery of this place on his way back from Tibet. Later, the Baishui became known as the holy land of the Dongba religion. Each year, on the eighth day of the second lunar month, the Naxi people gather here to celebrate their traditional festival by singing and dancing.

6 CAMARGUE

The Camargue lies at the mouth of the River Rhone, France. Camargue is Western Europe's largest river delta. It has an area of 300 square miles (780 sq km). Camargue is home to a specialised breed of bull, horses and pink flamingoes. Other animals include sheep, wild boar, beavers, badgers, tree frogs, water snakes, pond turtles. There are some 400 types of birds found here. There are a number of species of insects including one of the most ferocious mosquitoes. It is a place with rich flora and fauna, wonderful parks and museums and a range of adventure activities. It is also a bird watcher's paradise.

7 METÉORA MONASTERIES

This group of monasteries is located in Thessaly, Greece. The name 'Metéora' is Greek for 'suspended in the air,' which perfectly describes these remarkable monasteries.

There were 24 monasteries. Each contained a church or two, monks' cells and a refectory. Now only six remain. The first ones were built for hermits and ascetic monks in order to isolate themselves from the rest of the world. Some more were built around the 14th and 15th centuries as a way to get shelter from the Ottoman invasion.

In 1988, the monasteries were added to the UNESCO World Heritage list.

8 KREMLIN

The Kremlin came into existence in 1156. It was initially constructed of wood. In the 14th century, it was rebuilt in white stone. And finally, it was rebuilt in red brick in the late 15th century by Italian architects. Since then, it has been repaired and altered on several occasions. Its architecture, thus, reflects its long history and includes a variety of styles, including Byzantine, Russian Baroque and classical. The structure is triangular in shape. The Moscow Kremlin was designated a UNESCO World Heritage Site in 1990.

9 DECEPTION ISLAND

It is an active volcano in the South Shetland Islands, off the Antarctic Peninsula. It is shaped like a horseshoe. Its unique landscape comprises barren volcanic slopes, steaming beaches and ash-layered glaciers. It is one of the only places in the world where vessels can sail directly into the centre of a restless volcano. It was a former Norwegian whaling station. The whaling station was abandoned during the Great Depression. One of the major attractions of the island is the penguins. The island has at least 18 species of moss and lichen.

10 OKAVANGO DELTA

The Okavango Delta is in Botswana. It is portrayed as 'the jewel' of the Kalahari. The delta is made up of a network of channels and lagoons. It covers an area of 15,993 square kilometres. It is the largest inland delta in the world.

The delta is home to some of the largest number of wildlife in Africa and is one of Africa's ultimate safari destinations.

There are more than 400 species of birds. Other wildlife includes lions, elephants, hyenas, wild dog, buffalo, hippo and crocodiles, antelopes and other smaller animals like the warthog, mongoose, spotted genets, monkeys, bush babies and tree squirrels.

11 MOUNT FUJI

Mount Fuji lies on the island of Honshu, Tokyo. Mount Fuji is also known as Fuji-san. It is the highest mountain in Japan rising to 12,388 feet (3776 m). According to legend, an earthquake created Fuji in 286 BC. Mount Fuji is named for the Buddhist fire goddess Fuchi and is sacred to the Shinto Goddess Sengen-Sama, whose shrine is found at the summit. It is the holiest of Japan's 'Three Holy Mountains.'

Every summer, thousands of pilgrims and tourists climb to the summit, many of them hiking throughout the night to witness the sunrise from the summit. Its last major eruption was in 1707. Every summer, more than 200,000 people climb to the top of Fuji.

12 PONTE VECCHIO

Ponte Vecchio is also known as the Old Bridge as it is one the oldest bridges of Florence. The bridge is characterised by the small houses that line both sides of the bridge. The bridge is built across the Arno River in Florence, Italy. Its builder was Taddeo Gaddi. The bridge was completed in 1345. Originally, the sides held food shops, but by the end of the 15th century, the shops were assigned to goldsmiths and silversmiths. The upper side of the bridge, known as the Vasariano corridor, was designed by Giorgio Vasari to link Palazzo Vecchio and the Uffizi Gallery to the Pitti Palace. It is one of the most famous attractions of Florence.

13 KUNSTHISTORISCHES MUSEUM

The Kunsthistorisches Museum is in Vienna. The museum first opened in 1891. It was commissioned by the then emperor of Austria-Hungary, Franz Joseph I. It houses some of the world's most famous paintings and art exhibits. The purpose of this new museum in Austria was to house the art collection of the Habsburgs. Some famous works to be found in the museum include Michelangelo's *Madonna of the Rosary, The Crowning with Thorns* and *David with the Head of Goliath;* Raphael's *Madonna in Green;* and works by Rubens, Rembrandt and Titian. It also houses Egyptian, Roman and Greek Art. The museum also has special exhibits from time to time from other museums around the world.

14 PURNULULU NATIONAL PARK

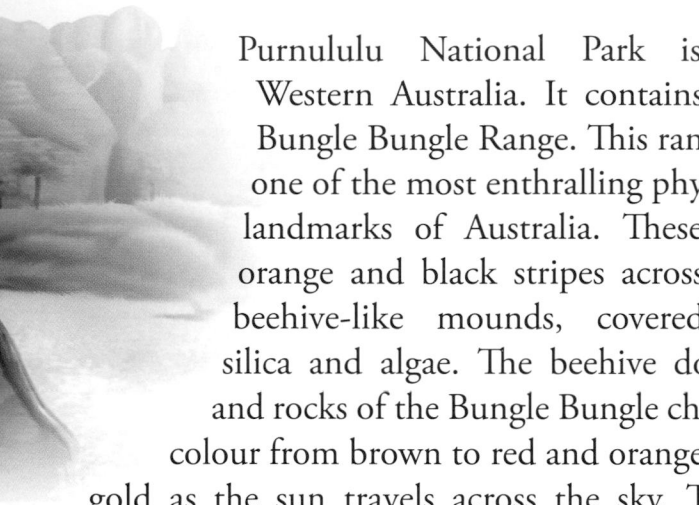

Purnululu National Park is in Western Australia. It contains the Bungle Bungle Range. This range is one of the most enthralling physical landmarks of Australia. These are orange and black stripes across the beehive-like mounds, covered in silica and algae. The beehive domes and rocks of the Bungle Bungle change colour from brown to red and orange and gold as the sun travels across the sky. These strange hillocks were the result of erosion over a period of 20 million years. The park is home to other natural phenomena including the Echidna Chasm, Cathedral Gorge and the soaring Piccaninny Gorge. Purnululu National Park was added to the World Heritage list in 2003 for these unique natural towers of sandstone.

15 WALT DISNEY WORLD

Walt Disney World is in Orlando, Florida. It is a recreational resort owned by the Walt Disney Company. The resort opened in 1971, with just the Magic Kingdom theme park. The resort is spread over an area of 30,500 acres, which makes it approximately the same size as San Francisco. There are four theme parks, two water parks, two night-time entertainment areas, over 20 hotels, six golf courses and much more. Miles of outdoor recreation are available including hiking, biking, boating and swimming. It has three separate areas containing shopping, dining and entertainment facilities as well as a fourth area with nightclubs. A fairly new addition to the resort is the state-of-the-art sports complex where Disney hosts a wide variety of sporting events. Approximately 48 million visitors make the trip to Orlando each year.

16 GRAND PLACE

Grand Place is in Brussels, Belgium. It is one of the most beautiful town squares in Europe. It dates back to the 11th century. There is a spectacular city hall, a Bread House, the King's House and a number of beautifully sculpted stone houses. This is the place where executions took place during the 15th century. UNESCO designated it as a World Heritage Site. Concerts and musical events are organised throughout the year on the square. The Flower Carpet is an event held every two years in August at the Grand Place. It involves the display of millions of fresh colourful begonias. The blooms are kept fresh for four days with the addition of fountains within the pattern on the carpet.

17 SCHÖNBRUNN PALACE

Schönbrunn Palace is in Vienna. It was the summer palace of the Habsburgs. The palace and its gardens were designated a UNESCO World Heritage Site in 1996. There are about 1440 rooms in the palace. The rooms are mostly decorated in the Rococo style. Other things to see are the Bohemian crystal chandeliers and white porcelain tile stoves. Schönbrunn Palace is Austria's most frequently visited tourist attraction Schönbrunn Tiergarten, perhaps the oldest zoo in Europe, was founded within the grounds in 1752. The entire complex covers more than 2 square kilometres.

18 FREDERIKSBORG CASTLE

Frederiksborg Castle is in Hillerød, Denmark. The oldest parts of the castle were built in 1560 by King Frederik II and the castle is named after him. The construction of the current palace started in 1602 and was completed in 1630. The construction comprised the building of three main wings and a fourth terrace lower wing. The style used was Renaissance with sweeping gables, sandstone decorations and copper-covered roofs and spires. The castle also houses the Museum of National History.

19 MONT SAINT-MICHEL

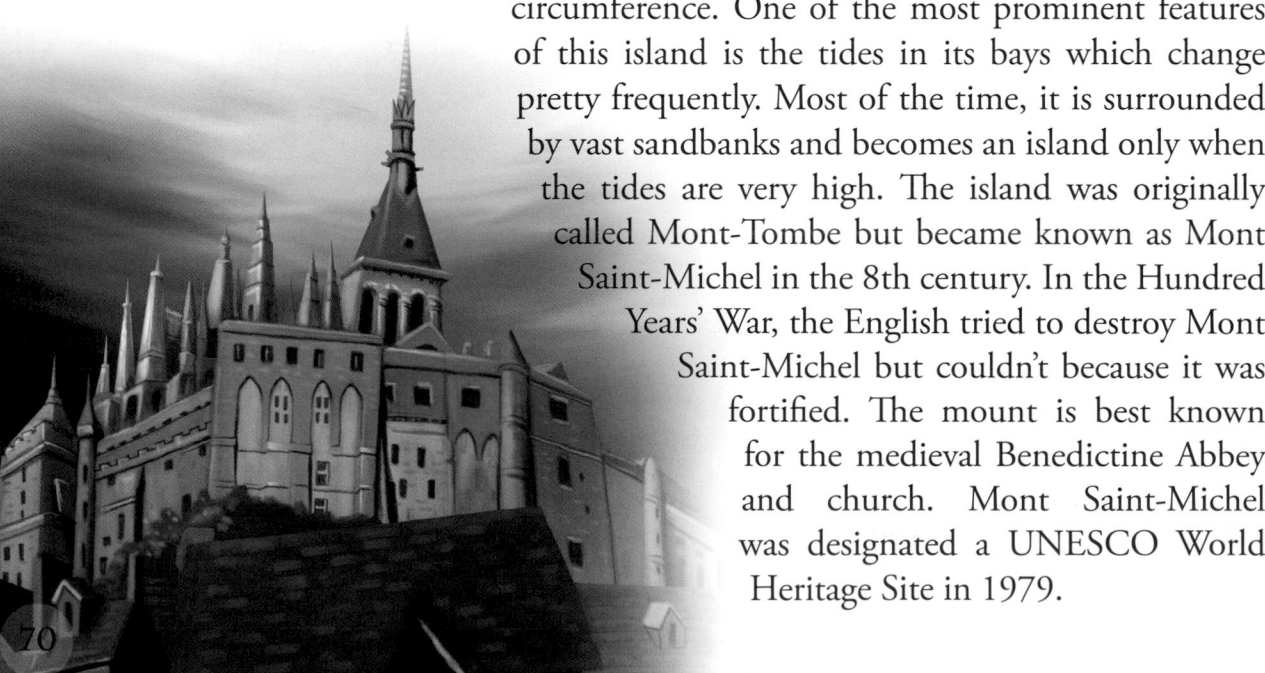

Mont Saint-Michel is in Normandy, France. It is a rocky islet. It is one of the popular tourist attractions in France. Mont Saint-Michel is almost circular, about 3000 feet in circumference. One of the most prominent features of this island is the tides in its bays which change pretty frequently. Most of the time, it is surrounded by vast sandbanks and becomes an island only when the tides are very high. The island was originally called Mont-Tombe but became known as Mont Saint-Michel in the 8th century. In the Hundred Years' War, the English tried to destroy Mont Saint-Michel but couldn't because it was fortified. The mount is best known for the medieval Benedictine Abbey and church. Mont Saint-Michel was designated a UNESCO World Heritage Site in 1979.

20 TREVI FOUNTAIN

The Trevi Fountain is in Rome. The fountain (Fontana di Trevi) is Rome's largest and most famous fountain. It stands 25.9 metres (85 ft) high and 19.8 metres (65 ft) wide. It was designed by Nicola Salvi in 1732 and competed in 1762. It is famous for its beautiful design and architecture. It depicts Neptune's chariot being led by Tritons with sea horses, one wild, one docile, representing the moods of the sea. The famous custom is to throw a coin into the fountain, thus ensuring your return to the Eternal City. You should toss it over your shoulder with your back towards the fountain.

21 UXMAL

Uxmal is an ancient city in Mexico. The name Uxmal means 'thrice visited' or 'thrice built.' It flourished between AD 600 and 900. It is one of the finest expressions of Mayan architecture known as the Puuc style. Characteristics of the Puuc style include limestone construction, often with smooth wall surfaces; plaster finishes; masks, etc. Other impressive structures are the Pyramid of the Magician, the Nunnery, and the Governor's Palace, with some 20,000 carved stone elements in its façade. Uxmal was designated a World Heritage Site in 1996.

22 WESTMINSTER ABBEY

The Westminster Abbey is in London. It is one of England's most important Gothic structures. Almost every English king and queen has been crowned in Westminster, and it is the burial place of 18 monarchs. England's most distinguished statesmen and famous subjects have been given burial in the Abbey since the 14th century. Some of them were Sir Isaac Newton, David Livingstone and Ernest Rutherford. Part of the south transept is well known as Poets' Corner and includes the tombs of Geoffrey Chaucer, Ben Jonson, John Dryden, Robert Browning and many others. In 1987, Westminster Abbey was designated a UNESCO World Heritage Site.

23 ANURADHAPURA

Anuradhapura is one of the ancient capitals of Sri Lanka. This sacred city was established around a cutting from the Buddha's fig tree, brought in the 3rd century BC. It is famous for its well-preserved ruins of ancient Lankan civilisation.

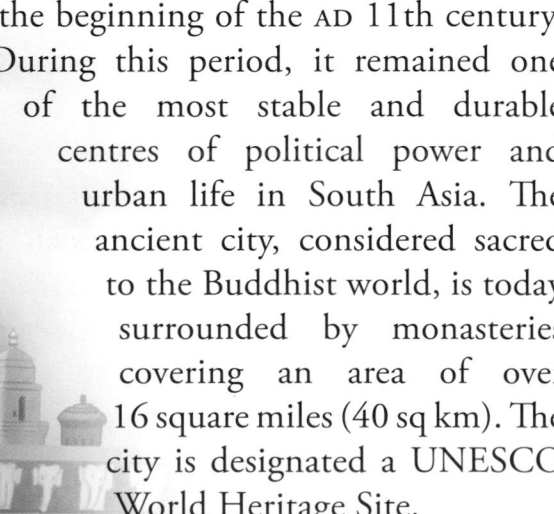

From the 4th century BC, it was the capital of Sri Lanka until the beginning of the AD 11th century. During this period, it remained one of the most stable and durable centres of political power and urban life in South Asia. The ancient city, considered sacred to the Buddhist world, is today surrounded by monasteries covering an area of over 16 square miles (40 sq km). The city is designated a UNESCO World Heritage Site.

24 TIKAL

Tikal is an ancient city of the Mayan civilisation in Guatemala. It is probably the largest and the oldest cities of the Maya civilisation. The most prominent structures in existence at the site are the Temple of the Jaguar, the Temple of the Mask, The Lost World Pyramid, The Great Plaza Ballcourt, Bat Palace and many Altars. It was designated a UNESCO World Heritage Site in 1979.

25 TEMPLE OF EMERALD BUDDHA

The Temple of Emerald Buddha is located in Bangkok. It is also known as Wat Phra Kaew. It is the most valued place of pilgrimage in Thailand. The Emerald Buddha statue is about 2 feet tall and is made of green jasper and covered with gold. A visit to Bangkok is not complete without a visit to this temple. The Emerald Buddha is covered in a seasonal costume, which is changed three times a year to correspond to the summer (crown and jewelry), winter (golden shawl), and rainy months (gilt robe and headdress).

The clothings which are not in use are kept on display in the Pavilion of Regalia, Royal Decorations and Thai Coins on the grounds of the Grand Palace. No one is allowed near the statue except the Thai king, who conducts rituals at the temple throughout the year.

26 TEMPLE OF ARTEMIS

The Temple of Artemis is in Ephesus, Turkey. It is one of the Seven Wonders of the Ancient World. The temple was dedicated to Artemis, the twin sister of Apollo. It was built by King Croesus of Lydia in about 550 BC. The size of the temple was over 350 feet by 180 feet. The temple was destroyed by the invading Goths in AD 262 and was never rebuilt. The Temple of Artemis was the first building made entirely of marble except for its tiled wooden roof. The temple was used as a marketplace and a religious institution. It was visited by merchants, tourists, artisans and kings who paid homage to the goddess by sharing their profits with her. Recent archeological excavations revealed gifts from pilgrims including statuettes of Artemis made of gold and ivory, earrings, bracelets and necklaces. The temple features many works of art like the four bronze statues of Amazon women.

27 CANTERBURY CATHEDRAL

The Canterbury Cathedral is in Canterbury, Kent. It is one of the oldest Christian churches in England. It was originally founded in AD 602 by St. Augustine. The cathedral has been designated a UNESCO World Heritage Site. It is the historic seat of the Archbishop of Canterbury. The Christ Church Gateway forms the main entrance into the Cathedral area. The figure of welcoming Christ at the centre is a present substitute of a statue destroyed during the Puritan Revolution. The central Bell Harry Tower is built of bricks and covered with stone. The elaborate carvings are characteristic of the late English Gothic style. There is a magnificent collection of medieval stained glass windows.

28 BAY OF FUNDY

Bay of Fundy is located on the Atlantic coast of North America, on the northeast end of the Gulf of Maine between the provinces of New Brunswick and Nova Scotia in Canada. The Bay of Fundy is 290 kilometres in length. The mouth of the bay is 100 kilometres wide and between 120 and 215 metres deep. It is a deep, funnel-shaped bay that splits at its northeastern head into the Chignecto Bay and the Minas Basin. The name 'Fundy' is thought to date back to the 16th century, when the Portuguese referred to the bay as 'Rio Fundo' or 'deep river'. The bay contains a diverse ecosystem featuring approximately eight species of whales, an abundance of dolphins, porpoises, fish, seals, and seabirds. The bay is surrounded by breathtaking cliffs, mud flats, and plateaus. Tides approaching a height of 17 metres, the highest in the world, occur in its eastern extremity.

29 HOOVER DAM

Hoover Dam is built on the Colorado River at the Arizona-Nevada border. It was once known as Boulder Dam. It was renamed in 1947 to honour President Herbert Hoover. Hoover Dam is the highest concrete dam in the western hemisphere, standing at more than 725 feet above the Colorado River. Its construction was completed in less than five years and well under budget in 1936. It has the world's largest hydroelectric power generating system with 17 generators producing 4 billion kilowatts of electricity every year, and it is still the largest hydroelectric power generator in the United States. It was also voted one of the top ten construction achievements of the 20th century. Besides being a major source of electrical power in the Southwest, Hoover Dam provides irrigation water to the neighbouring agricultural areas and helps in controlling floods in the area.

30 DRAKENSBERG

The Drakensberg mountain range is in South Africa. The range rises to more than 11,400 feet (3475 m). The local Zulu name for Drakensberg is Quathlamba which means 'the Barrier of Spears'. There are many game reserves and parks within the range. Rock paintings of the Bushmen can be seen in many parts of the Drakensberg. It is the main watershed of South Africa and is the source of the Orange River. The Drakensberg Park was designated a UNESCO World Heritage Site in 2000.

Did You Know?

- Niagara Falls is a great location for rainbows (or solar bows) which are created when the sunlight reflects off the Niagara Falls mist.
- Approximately 600 of the over 4700 archeological sites found in Mesa Verde National Park are cliff dwellings. Other sites include mesa top pueblos, farming terraces, towers, reservoirs and check dams.

1 STATUE OF LIBERTY

The Statue of Liberty Enlightening the World was a gift of friendship from the people of France to the people of the United States on the centenary of American independence in 1886 and is a universal symbol of freedom and democracy. French sculptor Frederic Auguste Bartholdi designed the Statue in collaboration with French engineer Gustave Eiffel.

It is a hollow colossus composed of thinly pounded copper sheets over a steel framework. The statue is 151 feet, 1 inch tall and was the tallest structure in the U.S. at the time it was built.

Visitors climb 354 steps (22 stories) to look out from 25 windows in the crown. They are strongly advised to wear comfortable shoes suitable for climbing small metal steps. The seven rays in the crown represent the Earth's seven seas.

2 ALTAMIRA CAVE PAINTINGS

The Altamira Cave Paintings are found in Spain. The Altamira site is one of the greatest collections of cave paintings ever discovered. The cave is 296 metres long and consists of a series of twisting passages and chambers shaped like the alphabet 'S'. The paintings depict the beginning of the Magdalenian period, about 15,000 years ago. Altamira was designated a UNESCO World Heritage Site in 1985. The cave was discovered by a hunter in 1868 and was visited in 1876 by Marcelino Sanz de Sautuola, a local nobleman. The paintings of bison, red deer, boar and horses date from 14,000 years ago, and were saved from the ruins of time and corrosion by an earlier landslide, which left them protected.

3 GANVIE

Ganvie is in Benin, Africa. The village is built on water. The houses stand on stilts and the people move around in small boats. Even the market is on water. According to a story, the people of Ganvie, in the 17th century, were escaping the Abomey kings and their brutal rule. Since the king's soldiers could not swim, they built themselves a village on the water, and were thereby safe from the persecutors. The main trade of the people there is fishing. It is a popular tourist attraction.

4 PALENQUE

Palenque is a ruined ancient Mayan city of southern Mexico. The most important structures at the site are El Palacio (the Palace), which has a tower that rises above the complex; Los Templos del Sol, de la Cruz, and de la Cruz Foliada (The Temples of the Sun, the Cross and the Foliated Cross). The city's ruins were designated a UNESCO World Heritage Site in 1987. The Temple of Inscriptions is famous for its hieroglyphic tablets and is one of the best-preserved Mayan temples. In 1952, a tomb was uncovered under the Temple of the Inscriptions, representing for the first time that the Maya pyramids served both as funerary structures and temple platforms.

5 MILFORD SOUND

Milford Sound is situated on the south-west of the South Island of New Zealand. It is named after Milford Haven. The fjord runs 15 kilometres inland from the Tasman Sea. It is considered to be New Zealand's most famous attraction. More than 5,50,000 people visit the fjord every year. The fjord is surrounded by towering rocks and mountains. Rainforests cover the cliffs and animals like seals, dolphins and penguins can be viewed. The sound is the northernmost fjord in Fiordland National Park. It is also the site of a town, Milford Sound, one of the region's few permanently inhabited places.

6 MAYON VOLCANO

Mayon Volcano is an active volcano. It is in Philippines. It is also known as Mount Mayon. It is well known for its shape, which is almost a perfect cone. There have been more than 30 eruptions recorded since 1616. Despite its volcanic activity, it is both a major tourist attraction and a land cultivated by farmers, because of its fertile slopes. The most recent eruption in 1993, began unexpectedly with an explosion and caused 75 deaths.

7 TUBBATAHA REEF MARINE PARK

The Tubbataha Reef Marine Park is spread over an area of 33,200 hectares in the middle of the Sulu Sea. It consists of the North and South Reefs and the adjacent Jessie Beazley Reef. The North islet of the park serves as a nesting ground for birds and marine turtles. The park is home to an amazing variety of marine life and features some of the most beautiful coral reefs in the world. Over one thousand species that can be found, many are already endangered species. Animal species found here include manta rays, lionfish, tortoise, clownfish, and sharks. It was designated a UNESCO World Heritage Site in 1993.

8 KHYBER PASS

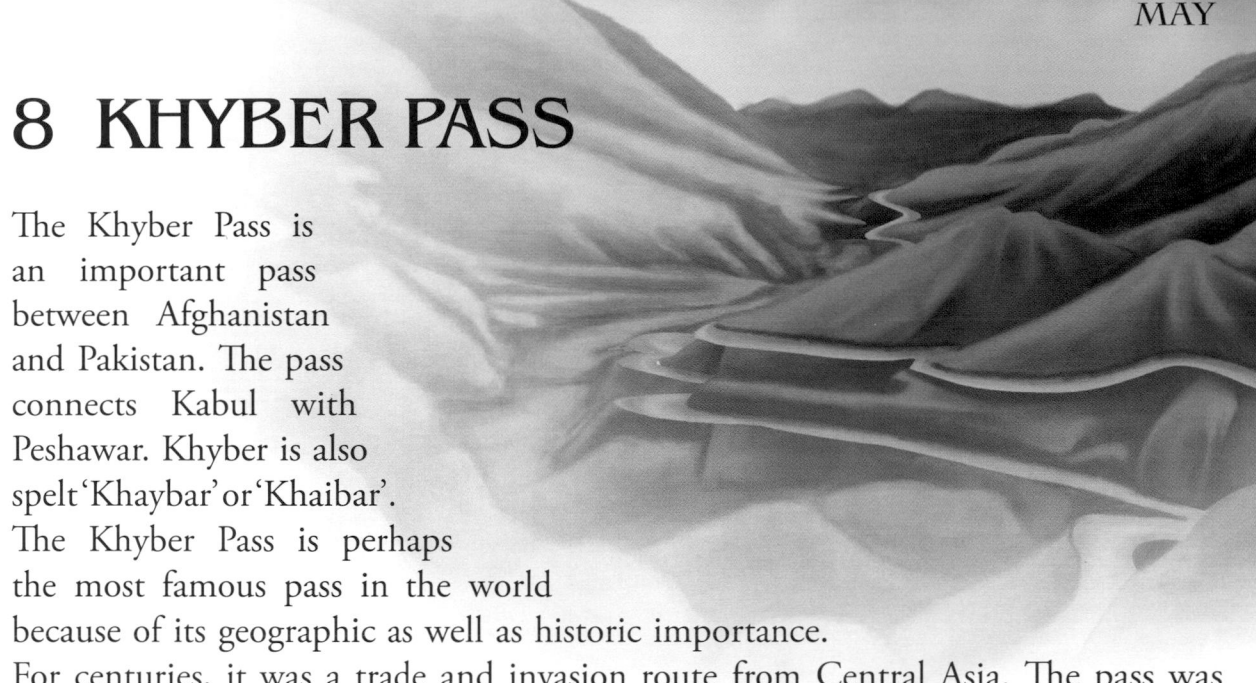

The Khyber Pass is an important pass between Afghanistan and Pakistan. The pass connects Kabul with Peshawar. Khyber is also spelt 'Khaybar' or 'Khaibar'. The Khyber Pass is perhaps the most famous pass in the world because of its geographic as well as historic importance.

For centuries, it was a trade and invasion route from Central Asia. The pass was one of the principal approaches of the armies of Alexander the Great, Timur, Babur, Mahmud of Ghazni and Nadir Shah during their invasions of India.

9 UPOLU

Upolu is an island of sand in Samoa in the South Pacific Ocean. The island is about 46 miles in length and 16 miles at its widest point with an area of 432 square miles (1119 sq km). The island's soil is fertile. Cacao, rubber, bananas and coconuts are grown here. Agriculture is the main occupation. Pigs, cattle and chickens are the most important livestock raised on the island. Besides agriculture, the people of Upolu are also engaged in industrial activities. Faleolo Airport offers both domestic and international air service to the island. The endangered flying fox and several types of tropical birds are found here.

10 TRULLI DISTRICT

Trulli District is in Apulia, Italy. The Trulli are one of the most unusual and unique structures in Italy. They are conical, stone-roofed houses. Fanciful, twisted chimneys decorate the rooftop of the houses. These buildings are built of a typical stone from the region. The walls are more than a metre thick, protecting the residents from heat and cold. Ladders leading to upper stories are present outside the houses. The houses are usually found in small clusters. Often, several Trulli are joined together to form a larger complex. The heart of the Trulli region is Alberobello, where there are more than 1000 Trulli built along the narrow streets. This Trulli-rich area of the town has been declared a national monument of Italy.

11 KIYOMIZU-DERA

Kiyomizu-dera (Pure Water Temple) is a Buddhist temple in eastern Kyoto, Japan. The temple was designated a UNESCO World Heritage Site in 1994. The main hall of Kiyomizu-dera is dedicated to Kannon, the Buddhist Goddess of compassion. It is famous for its vast *verandah*, supported by 139 wooden pillars (each 49 ft high), which juts out over the hillside and offers beautiful views of the city. The Kiyomizu Temple was founded in AD 780 and rebuilt in 1633. In Japanese, 'kiyoi mizu' means pure water. Drinking the water of the three streams that fall into a pond in the temple complex is said to confer wisdom, health, and longevity.

12 CATACOMBS OF ST. CALLIXTUS

The Catacombs of St. Callixtus are situated outside the city of Rome. The catacombs are ancient underground cemeteries used by the Christian and the Jewish communities. The first large-scale Christian catacombs were excavated in the AD 2nd century. They are 7 to 19 metres below the surface. Narrow steps join the multiple levels. There are some paintings, sculptures and epigraphs which can be found here and some of the original marble tablets are still preserved today. In addition to burial, the catacombs were used for memorial services and celebrations of the anniversaries of Christian martyrs.

13 METEOR CRATER

Meteor Crater is in Arizona, U.S. It is also called Barringer Meteorite Crater, Coon Butte, Arizona Meteor Crater or Canyon Diablo. The crater is a rimmed, bowl-shaped pit produced by a large meteorite. The crater is 4000 feet (1200 m) in diameter and about 600 feet (180 m) deep inside its rim, which rises nearly 200 feet (60 m) above the plain. It was discovered in 1891. It is estimated to be between 5000 and 50,000 years old. It is the best-preserved crater on Earth and a popular tourist attraction.

14 AGRIGENTO

Agrigento is a city situated in Sicily, Italy. The city of Agrigento was established in the 5th century bc by the Greeks. It is well-known for a number of archaeological structures. The plateau site of the city is rich in Greek remains. Some important ruins are the Valley of the Temples, Castle of Poggio Diana, Roman Temple of Olympian Zeus and the Fallen Atlas. Some prominent buildings of the medieval and modern city include the 14th-century cathedral, the 13th-century Churches of Santo Spirito and Santa Maria dei Greci, Baroque churches and palaces, and the rich archaeological museum. Agriculture is the main occupation of Agrigento. The world's best strawberries are available here.

15 NIAGARA FALLS

Niagara Falls is said to be the biggest waterfall on the River Niagara. The waterfall is located between two cities: Niagara Falls, Ontario and Niagara Falls, New York. The Niagara Falls is 27 kilometres (17 miles) long from the north to the northwest of Buffalo, New York and 120 kilometres (75 miles) long from south to southeast of Ontario. It is known both for its splendour and also as the source of hydraulic power. The Niagara Falls is called one of the most romantic places on Earth. The Falls at Niagara are about 12,000 years old. There are two parts of this fall: the American Falls and Niagara Falls, Canada usually called Horseshoe Falls. Between them is Goat Island, a tree-covered islet in the middle of the river. The Horseshoe Falls is on the Canadian side of the border. They are supposed to be the best and the most beautiful falls. The name of the falls has been derived due to the shape of the falls. The American Falls is a little less impressive than the Horseshoe as it has almost nine times less water in it and that is way it is not very striking to see.

16 CALAKMUL

Calakmul is a significant Maya site in Mexico. It is also called the 'City of the Two Adjacent Pyramids'. A snake head emblem has been found on all the artefacts of this region. At its height, during the Classic Mayan Period, the city is thought to have been home to 50,000 people. Of the 6750 ancient structures found at the site, the largest is the great pyramid. It is 55 metres high. It is the tallest of the Maya pyramids.

Other noteworthy structures on the site include 117 stelae, many of which come in pairs, as monuments to Mayan rulers and their wives. The city is also known for its murals which, unlike many other known examples, show scenes from all levels of society. It was designated a UNESCO World Heritage Site in 2002.

17 SUN TEMPLE

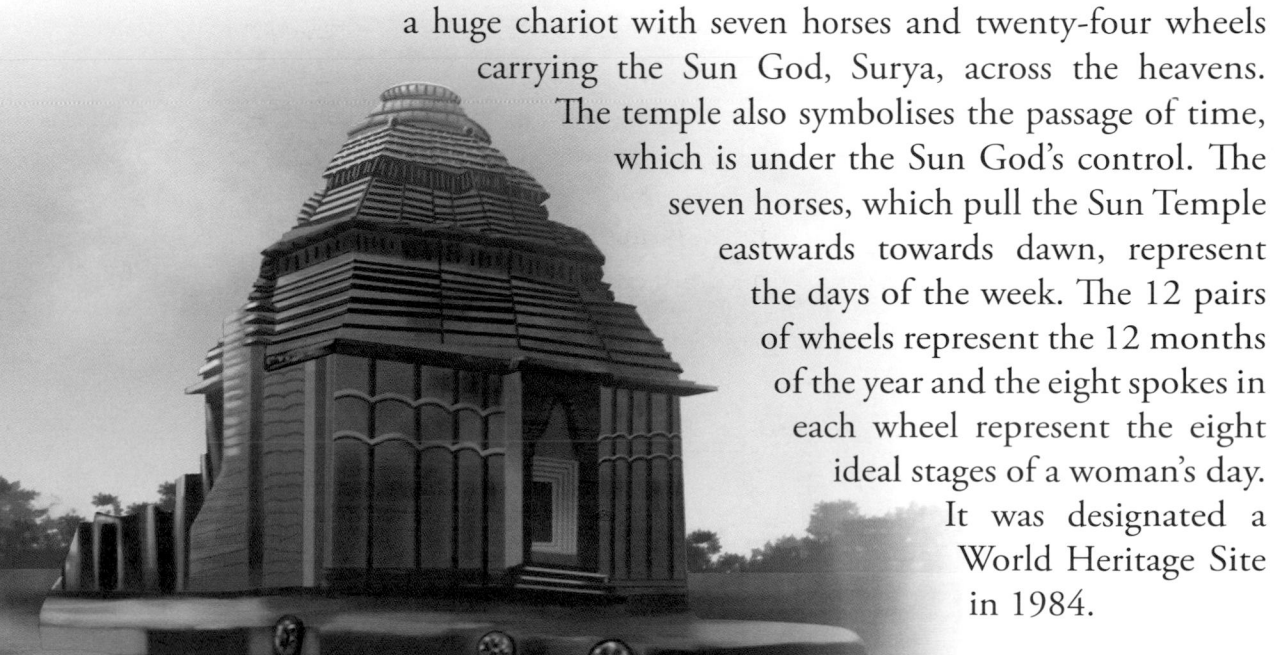

The Sun Temple of Konark is in Orissa, India. It was constructed in the 13th century by King Narasingh Deva. The entire temple was designed in the shape of a huge chariot with seven horses and twenty-four wheels carrying the Sun God, Surya, across the heavens. The temple also symbolises the passage of time, which is under the Sun God's control. The seven horses, which pull the Sun Temple eastwards towards dawn, represent the days of the week. The 12 pairs of wheels represent the 12 months of the year and the eight spokes in each wheel represent the eight ideal stages of a woman's day. It was designated a World Heritage Site in 1984.

18 DINGLE PENINSULA

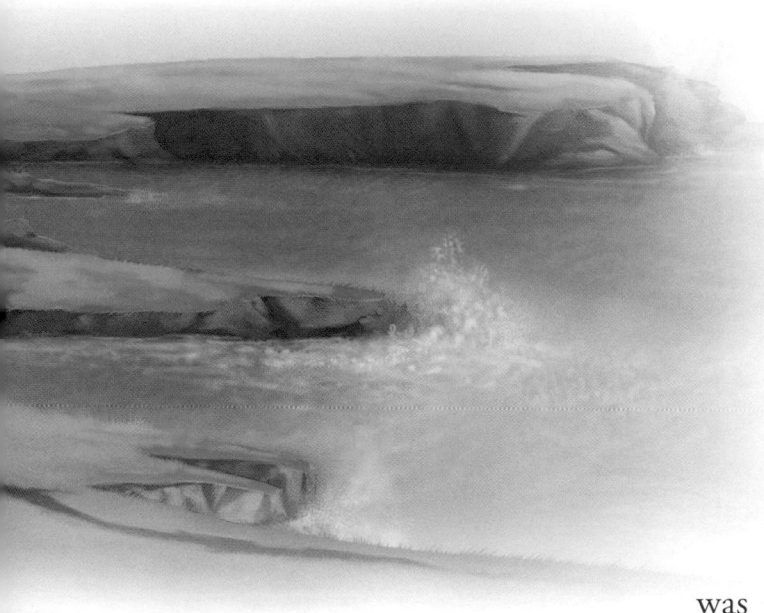

The Dingle Peninsula or Corca Dhuibhne is in Ireland. The peninsula is dominated by a range of mountains. The coastline consists of steep sea cliffs, broken by sandy beaches, with two large sand spits at Inch in the south and the Maharees to the north. It has a diving centre, sailing club, art galleries, craft shops and excellent accommodation. It was once cited as 'the most beautiful place on Earth' by the National Geographic. The hills and pastures are covered with beautiful green grass. The sight of the rocky shores and fishing villages in this area are stimulating and have a soothing effect on visitors' senses.

19 PANTHEON

The Pantheon is a building in Rome. It was built by Marcus Agrippa and rebuilt by Emperor Hadrian in AD 126. The Pantheon is remarkable for its size, construction and design. The dome measured about 142 feet (43 m) in diameter and rose to a height of 71 feet (22 m) above its base. The temple was converted into a Catholic Church in AD 609. Remarkably well preserved, it is mainly made of bricks with a great hemispherical dome whose supporting walls are set in concrete.

20 MESA VERDE NATIONAL PARK

Mesa Verde National Park is in southwestern Colorado. It was established in 1906 to preserve the prehistoric cliff dwellings. Mesa Verde offers a spectacular look into the lives of the Ancestral Pueblo people who made it their home for over 700 years, from AD 600 to 1300. Today, the park protects over 4000 known archeological sites, including 600 cliff dwellings. These sites are some of the most notable and best preserved in the United States. It was designated a World Heritage Site in 1978.

21 PERCÉ ROCK

Percé Rock is on the Gaspe Peninsula in Canada. It is one of the largest and most spectacular natural arches in the world. It is 1420 feet (433 m) long, 300 feet (90 m) wide, and 290 feet (88 m) high. Percé Rock is nearly 400 million years old and is embedded with countless fossils. The hole in the rock gave the wonder its name ('*percé*' means pierced in French). Percé is pronounced 'per-say'.

22 LIJIANG

Lijiang is located in Yunnan, China. The Old Town of Lijiang dates back to more than 800 years. The Old Town was designated a UNESCO World Heritage Site in 1997. It has an orderly system of waterways and bridges. The traditional residents of the Old Town are called the Nakhi people and have a culture, history and even architecture that is different from the rest of China. It has many famous places like the Mu Mansion, Jade Water Village, Lugu Lake and Dongba. The city is a major tourist destination.

23 NYMPHENBURG PALACE

The Nymphenburg Palace or Nymph's Castle is a baroque palace in Munich, Bavaria, Germany. The palace was the main summer residence of the rulers of Bavaria. The Baroque structure was begun in 1664 by the Prince Elector Maximilian II Emanuel. The circular Hall of Mirrors with silver ornament on a blue background and the symbolic hunting scenes is quite unique. The Nymphenburg gardens have been converted into a public park. The Botanical Garden in the Nymphenburg Park is one of the most beautiful gardens in Germany.

24 AITUTAKI ATOLL

Aitutaki is one of the Cook Islands north of Rarotonga. It is known as one of the most heavenly places on Earth. The island of Aitutaki is considered to be home to one of the most beautiful lagoons in the world. The crystal clear lagoon is the main highlight of visiting Aitutaki Island—the second most visited destination in the Cook Islands. Aitutaki Atoll is volcanic in origin and rises to about 450 feet (140 m).

25 REED FLUTE CAVE

Reed Flute Cave is located in the Guilin City, China. It is known as the Palace of Natural Arts as well. The cave is named after a type of reed growing outside from which melodious flutes are made. The cave is filled with a large number of stalactites, stalagmites and rock formations in wonderful shapes. The cave is about 240 metres long. There are 77 stone inscriptions covering many years of history. The cave was opened to public in 1962.

26 FONTAINEBLEAU

Fontainebleau is in Paris, France. Its château is one of the largest residences built by the kings of France. The Gallery of Francis I, the horseshoe exterior staircase, the ballroom and the council chamber are some of the things to see. The château is surrounded by pleasant gardens crossed by a canal built in the reign of Henry IV. It is protected by France's Office National des Forêts, and it is recognised as a French national park. The château at Fontainebleau has architectural elements from the 16th to the 19th century. The national forest of Fontainebleau is one of the most picturesque in France.

27 ZWINGER

The Zwinger (*Der Dresdner Zwinger*) is a palace in Dresden, Germany. It is a major landmark of German baroque architecture. The construction of the palace began in 1709 and was completed in 1719. Its construction was ordered by Augustus II, king of Poland, as a place for entertainments, tournaments and royal festivities. Its architect was Matthäus Daniel Pöppelmann. The name 'Zwinger' is taken from the German word '*Zwinger*' meaning the outer ward of a concentric castle. The Zwinger includes six pavilions connected by large galleries. The most impressive pavilions are the Rampart Pavilion (wall) and the Glockenspiel (carillon) Pavilion. The best-known feature of the Zwinger is the Kronentor or Crown Gate—a baroque gate topped by a large crown.

28 MEDICI CHAPEL

The Medici Chapel is in the New Sacristy of the Church of San Lorenzo in Florence, Italy. It contains the tombs of members of the Medici family. The monuments were commissioned in 1520 by Pope Clement VII. It was designed and built largely by Michelangelo and his students between 1520 and 1534.

29 DAZU ROCK CARVINGS

The Dazu Rock Carvings are a set of Buddhist sculptures carved in stone cliffs in Dazu, China. There are over 50,000 sculptures with over 100,000 Chinese characters of inscriptions and epigraphs. All the rock carvings can be viewed in normal light and are connected by walkways and paths. The two main sites are Bei Shan and Baoding Shan. They were designated a UNESCO World Heritage Site in 1999. Some sculptures are small, some are huge; many are brightly painted and portray religious and historical stories.

30 OLOMOUC

Olomouc city is in Czech Republic. It dates back to AD 10th century when it became an important trade crossing point. It has a noteworthy collection of historical monuments. The second oldest university in the Czech lands was founded in Olomouc in the year 1573. Olomouc's historic buildings include the 14th-century Gothic St. Wenceslas' Cathedral, the town hall and a 15th-century astronomical clock. Olomouc is also known for its fountains, notable among which are Triton (1707) and Caesar's (1720).

31 NIMES AMPHITHEATRE

Nimes Amphitheatre is in Nimes, France. It was built at the end of the first century. It measures about 133 metres in length and 101 metres in width. The façade is at a height of 21 metres and consists of two levels of 60 arches each. Inside this, more than 20,000 spectators could attend the fights of the gladiators. A complicated system of corridors and stairs allowed to each of the spectator to quickly reach their place or to leave the building at the end of the performances. It has a capacity of 16,300 spectators.

Did You Know?

- Teotihuacan was named thus by the Aztecs, centuries after its destruction. The name means "birthplace of the gods."
- The Forbidden City in China has the world's largest collection of preserved ancient wooden structures.

1 PYRAMIDS OF GIZA

The Pyramids of Giza are in Egypt and are the most famous monuments of ancient Egypt. These massive stone structures were built around 4500 years ago. They are the only wonders of the ancient world still standing. The Pyramids of Giza consist of three pyramids: the Great Pyramid of Khufu, the Great Pyramid of Khafre and the Great Pyramid of Menkaure. The Pyramid of Khufu is 230.364 metres square at the base and 137.18 metres high. The Pyramid of Khafre is 215.8 metres square at the base and 136.5 metres high. The Pyramid of Menkaure is 108.5 metres square at the base and 66.5 metres high.

The Pyramid of Khufu is also known as the Great Pyramid. The Great Pyramid is truly an astonishing work of engineering skill—for over four thousand years, until the modern era, it was the tallest building in the world. It was constructed using around 2,300,000 limestone blocks, weighing, on an average, 2.5 tons each, although some weighed as much as 16 tons. The ancient ruins of the Memphis area, including the Pyramids of Giza, were collectively designated a World Heritage Site in 1979. The pyramids are amongst the most famous tourist attractions in the modern world.

2 NUKU HIVA

Nuku Hiva is the largest of the Marquesas Islands in French Polynesia. It is considered to be the most beautiful island. Nuku Hiva is a volcanic island. There are eight harbours, the best being the Taiohae Bay. Copra is the chief export.

3 PARADISE ISLAND

Paradise Island is in the Bahamas. Paradise Island was once known as Hog Island and it was a major site for farming in the Bahamas. Hog Island became Paradise Island when it was purchased by Huntington Hartford in 1959.

4 LEMAIRE CHANNEL

Lemaire Channel is one of Antarctica's most popular tourist destinations. It is found between rocky Booth Island and the mountainous western coast of the Antarctic Peninsula. It is 11 kilometres long and 1600 metres wide at its narrowest point. The place is a perfect destination for cruising in Antarctica. Glacial calving is a common occurrence along the banks of the channel. Penguins and seals can be found here. Lemaire Channel has been nicknamed 'Kodak Gap' due to the number of photographs taken by the visitors while passing through it.

5 LI RIVER CRUISE

The Li River is in Guangxi. The cruise is one of the most scenic cruises on earth. The river cruises usually start in the morning from Guilin and arrive at Yangshuo after lunch. The entire journey lasts about four hours. With its breathtaking scenery along the Li River, the cruise has become one of China's top tourist destinations. One comes across the following: Elephant-Trunk Hill, Rooster Fighting Hill, Pagoda Hill, Forest of Odd-Shaped Peaks, Daxu Ancient Town and Ox Gorge.

6 CABOT TRAIL

The Cabot Trail is in Nova Scotia, Canada. The trail loops around the northern tip of Cape Breton Island. It is 185 miles long. The trail passes through breathtaking sceneries. The Cape Breton Highlands National Park lies along the Cabot Trail, and provides world-class hiking. The Cabot Trail is considered one of the world's most scenic destinations. It is named after the famous explorer John Cabot.

7 LIGHTHOUSE OF ALEXANDRIA

The Lighthouse of Alexandria was constructed on the island of Pharos in Alexandria, Egypt. The entire structure was about 400 feet tall including the base. It was destroyed in an earthquake in the 1300s. The light on the top of the lighthouse could be seen for 35 miles. There was a mirror on the top of it that reflected the light. A staircase in the lighthouse led the keepers to the beacon chamber. The Lighthouse of Alexandria was one of the Seven Ancient Wonders of the World. It was built by Sostratus and completed in about 280 BC.

8 TALLINN

Tallinn is the capital and largest city of Estonia. It occupies an area of 159.2 square kilometres (61.5 sq miles) with a population of 4,06,703. It is one of the best-retained European towns, especially the Old Town, with its unique medieval surroundings. The Old Town was designated a UNESCO World Heritage Site in 1997.

9 KENNEDY SPACE CENTER

The Kennedy Space Center is located in Brevard County on Florida's east coast. The actual spaceport and launch facilities are located at Cape Canaveral. The Kennedy Space Center is one of the ten NASA centers that serves as America's spaceport. Space shuttle launches are visible from miles around and draw thousands of visitors. The Kennedy Space Center Visitor Complex offers tours of the launch area, views of the giant rockets and even lunch with an astronaut. The Kennedy Space Center is 55 kilometres long, 10 kilometres wide and covers an area of 570 square kilometres.

10 RHINE GORGE

The Rhine Gorge is a 65-kilometre section of the River Rhine between Koblenz and Bingen in Germany. The rocks in the Rhine Gorge are said to be 416–360 million years old. The remnants of the rock structures consist mainly of slate. From this area, an amazing view of the Rhine Gorge valley can be seen. The climate at the Rhine Gorge differs from one region to another. For this reason, a wide variety of species are found in this region. It was designated a UNESCO World Heritage Site in 2002.

11 GOLDEN TEMPLE

The Golden Temple is located in the city of Amritsar, India. It was established by Guru Ram Dasji, the fourth guru of the Sikhs. It is informally referred to as Harmandir Sahib. It is considered the holiest shrine by the Sikhs. It is a symbol of both beauty and peace. The temple is surrounded by a small manmade lake. The temple was built with four doors to show that every religion or faith is allowed to go in to meditate or just listen to the prayers for peace. The entire top of the Golden Temple is made of pure gold and thus adds a lot of pride and beauty to the entire temple.

12 ZION NATIONAL PARK

Zion National Park is in Utah. It is Utah's oldest national park covering about 229 square miles. It is known for its incredible canyons which attract nearly three million visitors each year. The main sections of the park are the Zion Canyon, Kolob Canyon, Kolob Terrace and Highway 9. Wildlife such as mule deer, golden eagles, and mountain lions, also inhabit the park. Zion offers probably the best, most varied hiking of all national parks, including the famous Narrows Trail along the upper stretches of the Virgin River. Zion has a variety of plants—more than 900 species—not found anywhere else in Utah.

13 CANALS OF VENICE

Venice is famous because of its canals. The canals date back to the 5th century. The city has about 150 canals and the most important canal in Venice is called the Grand Canal. It is responsible for managing the traffic in water through corridor management. It is very common to find water buses and water taxis as means of transport. The city has almost 400 bridges. The total length of the Grand Canal is 3 kilometres. The Grand Canal is lined on either side by palaces, churches, hotels and other public buildings. The styles used are Romanesque, Gothic and Renaissance.

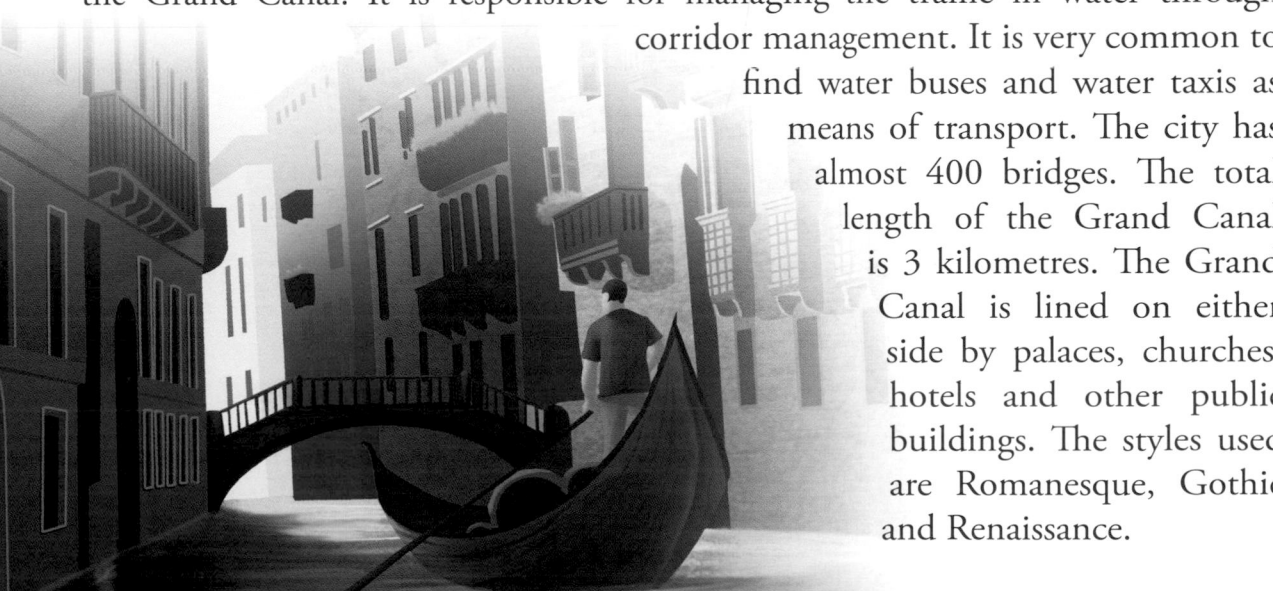

14 MEDINA OF FEZ

The Medina of Fez is in Morocco. It was designated a UNESCO World Heritage Site in 1981. The Medina of Fez is a beautiful place with grand historical buildings that date back to medieval times. These well-preserved buildings include mosques, palaces, fountains and residential homes. The oldest university in the world is also located in the Medina of Fez. It is impossible to find one's way through the closely built shops and houses on the tangled streets that can be called a maze. These old buildings are surrounded by 8 kilometres of fortified walls that were built in an attempt to keep invaders out of the city. Today, a number of the ancient houses are available to tourists on rent for a holiday.

15 TRINITY COLLEGE LIBRARY

The Trinity College Library is the largest research library in Ireland. The Long Room, the main room of the library, houses Ireland's largest collection of books and manuscripts. Its main treasure is the Book of Kells, one of the great masterpieces of early Christian art. Other special collections include the Ussher Collection acquired in 1661, the Fagel Collection of 1802, the Book of Armagh, a 9th-century copy of the New Testament that also contains St. Patrick's Confession and the legendary Book of Durrow, a 7th-century gospel book. The Long Room is 213 feet long and 42 feet wide. It contains approximately 200,000 of the 3 million volumes in Trinity's collection. It has an impressive series of marble busts, of which the most famous is that of Jonathan Swift.

16 UFFIZI GALLERY

The Uffizi Gallery is in Florence, Italy. It is one of the oldest and most famous art museums of the world. It has the world's finest collection of Italian Renaissance paintings. It also has antiques, sculpture and more than 100,000 drawings and prints. The Uffizi Gallery has a huge collection of Florentine paintings from the late Gothic through the Renaissance and Mannerist periods, including masterpieces by Botticelli, Mantegna and Leonardo da Vinci.

17 HOFBURG PALACE

Hofburg Palace is in Vienna, Austria. It currently serves as the Austrian Federal President's official seat. It was the Habsburg's principal winter residence. The palace has been expanded over the centuries according to the needs and demands of various ruling families and the government. It now includes various residences, the chapel, museums, the Imperial Library, the treasury, the national theatre, the riding school, the horse stables and the Hofburg Congress Center. The styles used were Italian and Baroque. The palace complex is quite large. There are some 2600 rooms in the palace.

18 GREAT BUDDHA OF KAMAKURA

The Great Buddha of Kamakura is in the city of Kamakura, Japan. It is a bronze statue of Amida Buddha. The statue is 13.35 metres high and weighs approximately 93 tons. It is the second largest monumental Buddha in Japan. The statue was probably built in 1252 inside a wooden temple. It seems that a huge tsunami washed away the wooden structure sometime in the late 15th century, and the statue has been in the open ever since. The Great Buddha is seated in the lotus position.

19 MONTEREY BAY AQUARIUM

Monterey Bay Aquarium is in Monterey, California. It was established in 1984. There are about 300,000 specimens of fish. There are 200 pools and galleries. The two most notable among its many tanks are the one showcasing Californian coastal marine life and the other, the Outer Bay Wing. The Outer Bay Wing was home to the first great white shark ever kept in an aquarium. The aquarium pumps 2000 gallons of Monterey Bay water through more than 100 exhibit tanks every day. There are telescopes, macroscopes and microscopes, and even underwater video cameras to view all the marine animals and vegetation of the bay.

20 PETRONAS TWIN TOWERS

The Petronas Twin Towers is in Kuala Lumpur, Malaysia. They held the record for being the world's tallest buildings for 6 years before being surpassed by Taipei 101 in 2004. Although they have lost the title of being the world's tallest buildings, Petronas are still the tallest twin buildings in the world. The towers were built by an Argentine-American architect, Cesar Pelli. The construction of the twin towers took 7 years and was completed in 1998. The towers house big shopping malls on their bottom floors. Each tower has 88 floors in it. The towers were designed to symbolise power and elegance using geometric principles typified in Islamic architecture.

21 TABLE MOUNTAIN NATIONAL PARK

The Table Mountain National Park is in Cape Town, South Africa. Earlier it was known as the Cape Peninsula National Park. The park protects the natural environment of the Table Mountain Chain, and in particular the rare fynbos vegetation. It is managed by the South African National Parks. The park comprises part of the Cape Floristic Region World Heritage Site. From an aerial view, the Table Mountain National Park resembles a narrow finger, featuring a variety of impressive beaches, bays and valleys. The park is bordered by the Atlantic Ocean on the west and False Bay on the east. Two of the most beautiful landmarks in the country can be found inside the park, the Cape of Good Hope and Table Mountain.

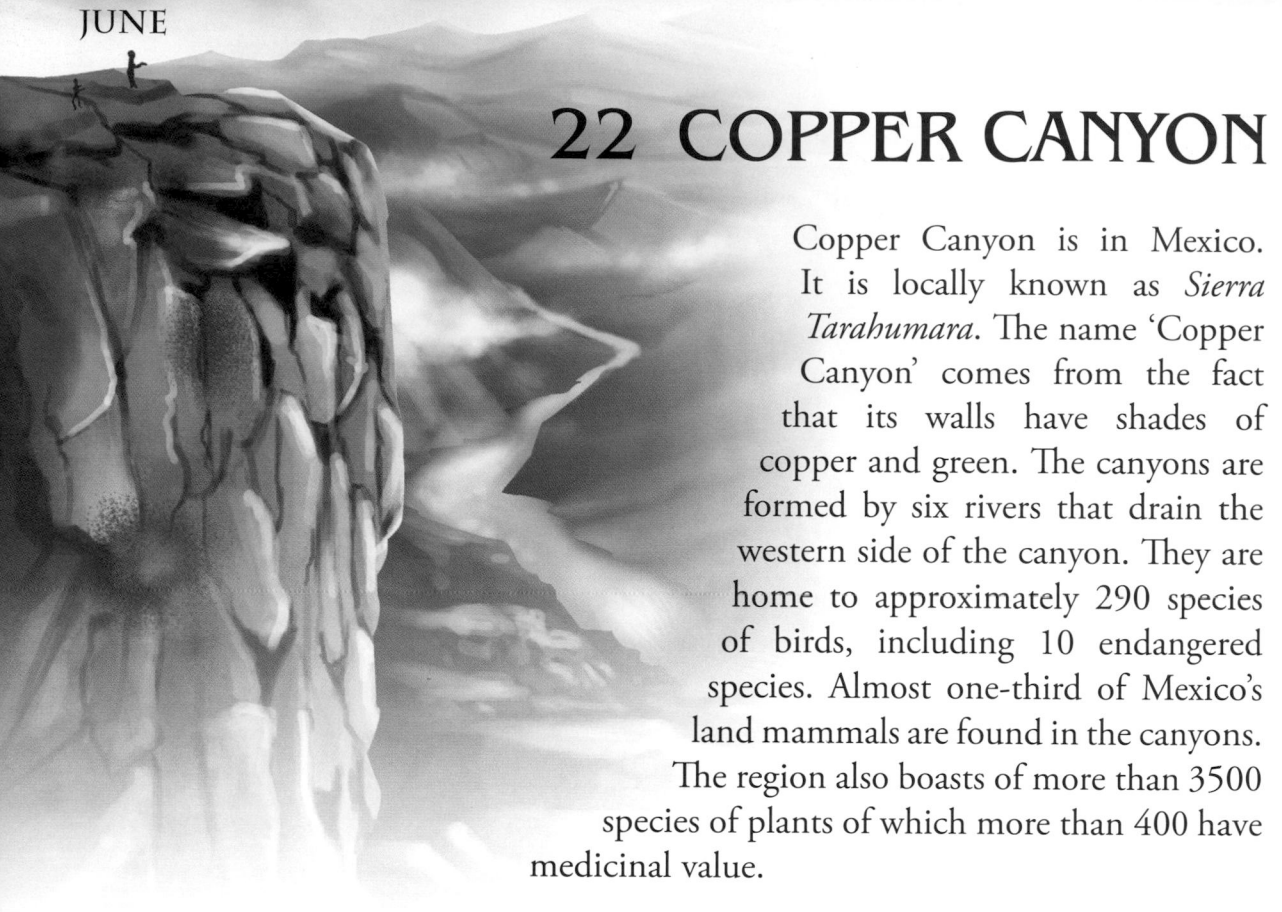

22 COPPER CANYON

Copper Canyon is in Mexico. It is locally known as *Sierra Tarahumara*. The name 'Copper Canyon' comes from the fact that its walls have shades of copper and green. The canyons are formed by six rivers that drain the western side of the canyon. They are home to approximately 290 species of birds, including 10 endangered species. Almost one-third of Mexico's land mammals are found in the canyons. The region also boasts of more than 3500 species of plants of which more than 400 have medicinal value.

23 MARRAKESH

Marrakech or Marrakesh also known as the Red City is in Morocco in the foothills of the Atlas Mountains. The peaks of the Atlas Mountains behind the city present a picturesque scene. Djamaa el Fna is the main square of the city. It is the world's most thrilling and lively gathering place. The city becomes very humid during summer and snowy during winter. The name 'Marrakesh' has originated from an Amazigh word 'Murnakush' which means Land of Gods. Marrakech has the largest traditional market in Morocco. The market is always busy and is packed with drummers, acrobats, storytellers, water sellers, dancers and musicians. The elegant 70 metre (230-ft) high Koutoubia minaret is Marrakesh's primary landmark.

24 PAMALICAN ISLAND

Pamalican Island is in Philippines. It is one of the nearly 1800 islands in the province of Palawan. The island is sprinkled with lush coconut trees and five kilometres of white sand beach. There are coral reefs that spread 50–300 metres from the shore. The turquoise sea is crystal clear and excellent for swimming, snorkelling, scuba diving, fishing and sailing. The island has the Amanpulo Resort, a quiet luxury resort for relaxation and peace.

25 OSTIA ANTICA

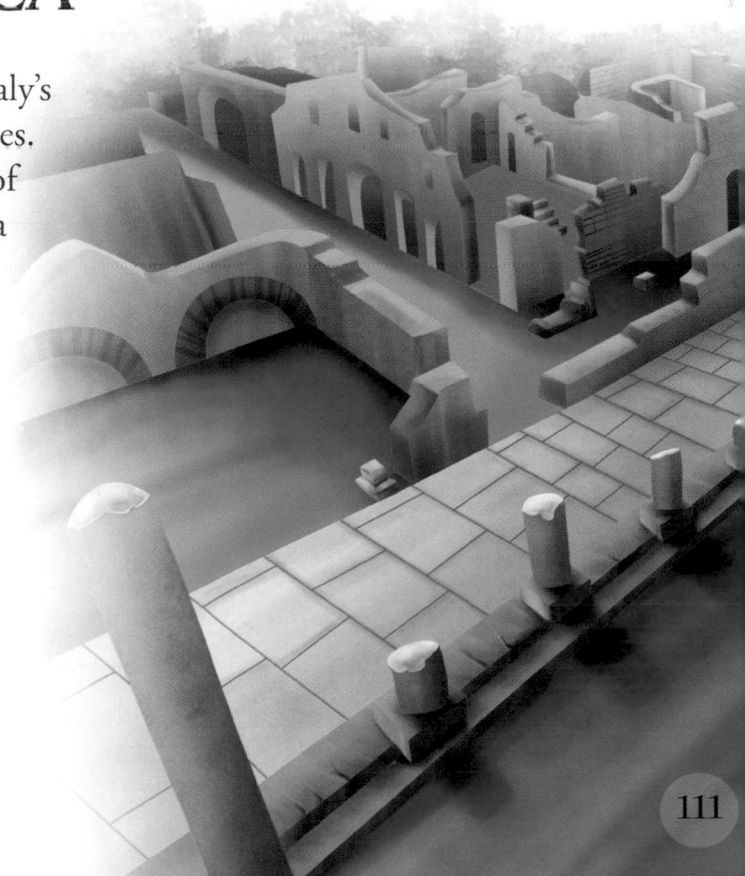

Ostia Antica is in Italy. It is one of Italy's best-preserved archaeological sites. The name 'Ostia' means 'mouth of the river' in Latin. Originally, Ostia was at the mouth of the Tiber River. Ostia is believed to have been founded during the 4th century BC as a military base. Ostia's prosperity reached its height in the early AD 2nd century. The town is noted for the excellent preservation of its ancient buildings and magnificent frescoes.

26 KRUGER NATIONAL PARK

The world-renowned Kruger National Park is in Africa. It covers nearly 2 million hectares and stretches from north to south along the Mozambique border. Its plant life includes baobabs, fever trees, knob thorns, marulas and mopane trees. Animals include lions, elephants, Cape buffaloes, leopards, rhinos, buffalo weavers, elephant shrews, leopard tortoises, and rare insects like the ant lion and rhino beetle. Notable among its numerous birds are the ground hornbill, kori bustard, lappet-faced vulture, martial eagle and saddle-bill stork.

27 SALISBURY CATHEDRAL

Salisbury Cathedral is in Salisbury, London. It was built in the 13th century. The Cathedral is a Gothic edifice. The construction began in 1220 and was completed by 1258. The cathedral has the tallest spire and the largest cloisters in England. Its towering central spire (404 feet tall) is the tallest in England. There are 332 steps that take one up the tower to glimpse the fine views of Salisbury and the surrounding countryside. The central garden is home to two giant cedar trees planted in 1837. The cathedral has Europe's oldest working clock which dates back to AD 1386. It is a centre of pilgrimage for thousands of visitors every year.

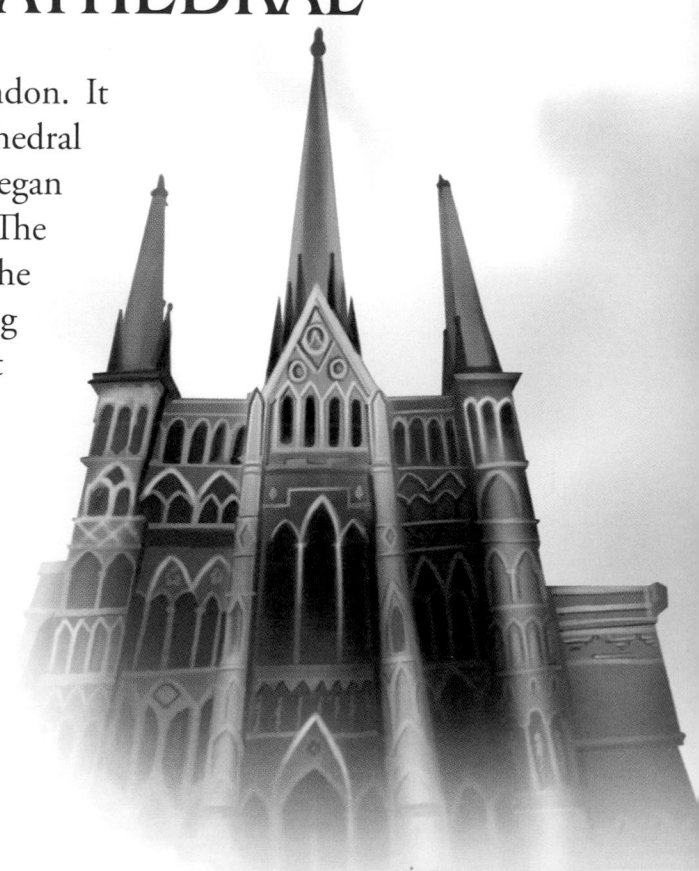

28 BOSRA THEATRE

Bosra Theatre is in Bosra, Syria. It is the largest and best-preserved of all Roman theatres in the Middle East. It was built in AD 2nd century after Bosra became the capital of the new Roman province of Arabia. In the Middle Ages, a Muslim fortress was built around the theatre, which explains its excellent maintenance. It could seat up to 15,000 people. The theatre now serves as the main venue for the Bosra National Music Festival.

29 IMPERIAL WAR MUSEUM

The Imperial War Museum is in the United Kingdom. The museum was founded in 1917 to keep a record of Britain's war effort and sacrifice and to display material relating to World War I. In 1939, the museum started collecting items from the World War II and eventually it began its current policy of exhibiting memorabilia from all British conflicts. The museum's collections include archives of personal and official documents, photographs and video recordings. It also houses an extensive library, a large art collection, samples of military vehicles and aircraft, and other equipments related to wars and international conflicts. The museum also holds special exhibitions.

30 KINGS CANYON NATIONAL PARK

Kings Canyon National Park is in southern Sierra Nevada, California. It was established in 1940. The park has an area of 722 square miles (1870 sq km). It contains groves of giant sequoias including Grant and Cedar groves. The park's most amazing feature is Kings Canyon. The canyons of the Kings River are actually the deepest canyons in North America, deeper even than the Grand Canyon. The park's forests also have sugar and yellow pine, white fir and incense cedar. Animals like deer, black bears, bighorn sheep, etc. are found here.

Did You Know?

- Angkor Wat was made as a Hindu Temple, with Vishnu as its chief God. Later it became a Buddhist temple.

- The ancient city of Bagan in Burma has been called Arimaddana (City of the Enemy Gusher), Tambadipa (Land of Copper) and Tassadessa (Parched Land).

1 CHICHÉN ITZÁ

Chichén Itzá is in Mexico. Chi means 'mouths', chén means 'wells' and Itzá the 'Itzá tribe'. It was an important Maya city until AD 10th century. After that the Maya civilisation declined and Toltec warriors seized and controlled Chichén Itzá. The remains at the site are neither Mayan nor Toltec but a mixture of both cultures. Chichén Itzá was thought to have been built for the god Kukulcan. El Castillo, a pyramid temple, was dedicated to him. The days and months of the year are represented on El Castillo by the number of steps and terraces. The early buildings are in an architectural style known as Puuc. These earliest structures include the Akabtzib (House of the Dark Writing), the Chichanchob (Red House), the Iglesia (Church), the Casa de las Monjas (Nunnery) and the observatory

El Caracol (The Snail). Chichén Itzá was designated a UNESCO World Heritage Site in 1988. It is one of Mexico's most-visited tourist destinations.

There was a well of sacrifice in Chichén Itzá. During drought, victims were thrown alive in the well to provoke the rain god into action. Many victims drowned but those who survived were treated with respect as they were believed to have communicated with the gods.

2 MUSEUM OF ANTHROPOLOGY

The Museum of Anthropology is located on the campus of the University of British Columbia, Canada. The museum was founded in 1949. The collections include materials from all continental areas. The museum houses some 36,000 ethnographic objects and 5,35,000 archaeological objects. In the museum's Great Hall are massive totem poles, carved boxes, bowls and feast dishes, while smaller pieces in gold, silver, argillite, wood, ceramic and other materials are exhibited elsewhere in the galleries.

3 CHENGDE MOUNTAIN RESORT

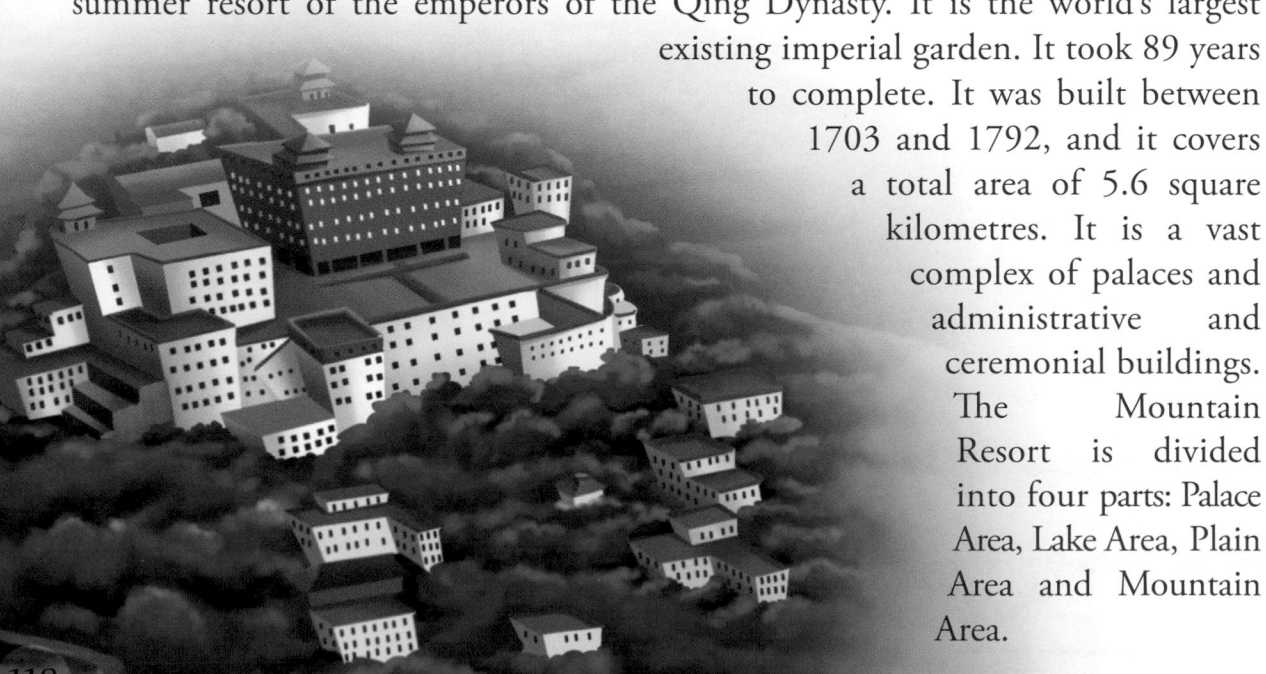

Chengde Mountain Resort is situated in the city of Chengde, China. It was the summer resort of the emperors of the Qing Dynasty. It is the world's largest existing imperial garden. It took 89 years to complete. It was built between 1703 and 1792, and it covers a total area of 5.6 square kilometres. It is a vast complex of palaces and administrative and ceremonial buildings. The Mountain Resort is divided into four parts: Palace Area, Lake Area, Plain Area and Mountain Area.

4 GREAT SPHINX

The Sphinx is in Giza, Egypt. The Great Sphinx is a large human-headed lion that was carved from a mound of natural rock. It is 73.5 metres (241 ft) long, 6 metres (20 ft) wide and 20.22 metres (66.34 ft) high. It was carved out of limestone. The Sphinx was built around 2530 BC by the Pharaoh Khafre. The Sphinx is thought to be primarily a guardian figure, protecting the tomb of the Khafre by warding off evil spirits.

5 KHAJURAHO

Khajuraho is in Madhya Pradesh, India. Khajuraho was one of the capitals of the Chandela kings, who ruled from the 9th to the 11th century. It originally had about 85 temples built by multiple rulers from about 950 to 1050. These temples are built in the North Indian Nagara style. The temples have an abundance of sculptures. Most of the temples are built of sandstone, with varying shades of buff, pink and pale yellow. Of the 85 original temples about 20 are still well preserved. The temples are divided into three complexes. The western is the largest and contains the splendid Shaivite temple, Kandariya Mahadev, 31 metres high. Khajuraho's name derives from the prevalence of 'khajur' or date palms in the area. Khajuraho was designated a UNESCO World Heritage Site in 1986.

6 DUBROVNIK

Dubrovnik is in Croatia. It is also called the 'Pearl of the Adriatic'. It is one of the most famous tourist spots. The city has been a town of notable poets, painters, politicians, playwrights and scholars. Dubrovnik is famous for its destinations like Roland's Column, the Bell Tower, the Sponza Place, War Photo Limited, Pile Gate and some churches and museums. The Old Town of Dubrovnik was designated a UNESCO World Heritage Site in 1979.

7 PRAGUE OLD TOWN

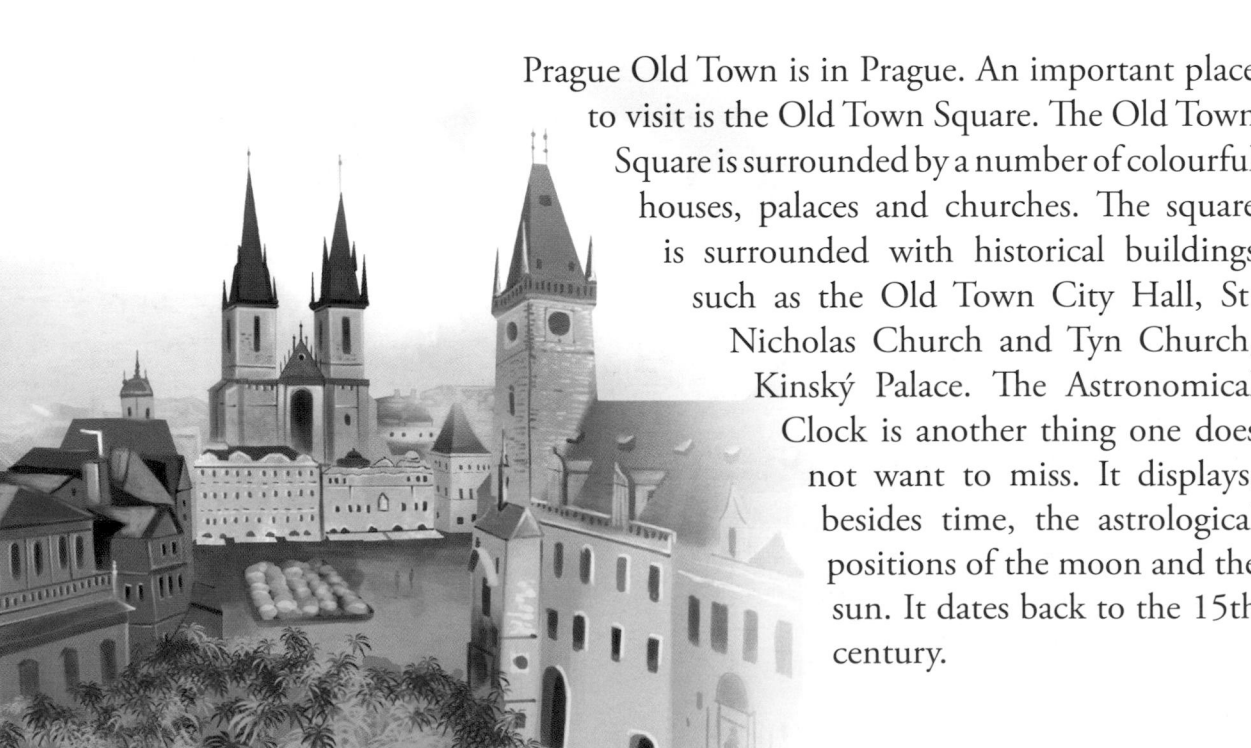

Prague Old Town is in Prague. An important place to visit is the Old Town Square. The Old Town Square is surrounded by a number of colourful houses, palaces and churches. The square is surrounded with historical buildings such as the Old Town City Hall, St. Nicholas Church and Tyn Church, Kinský Palace. The Astronomical Clock is another thing one does not want to miss. It displays, besides time, the astrological positions of the moon and the sun. It dates back to the 15th century.

8 CESKY KRUMLOV

Cesky Krumlov is in Czech Republic. There are two main attractions of Cesky Krumlov. One is the Cesky Krumlov Castle and the other is the Cesky Krumlov Old Town. The castle dates back to the 13th century. It is situated on a hill. The castle has Gothic, Renaissance and Baroque elements. The castle area is a complex of 40 buildings and palaces, situated around five castle courts and a castle park spanning an area of 7 hectares. Cesky Krumlov was designated a UNESCO World Heritage Site in 1992.

9 CHAMBORD CHATEAU

The Chambord Chateau is at Chambord, France. The chateau was built by King Francois I in the 16th century, in the Renaissance style. Its main purpose was to serve as a country palace and also as a hunting lodge. It is the largest castle in the Loire Valley. The castle has 440 rooms, 365 fireplaces and 84 staircases. It is so big that not even 365 fireplaces were enough to keep it warm in winter. One of the architectural delights is the stunning double-helix open staircase in the castle. People coming down the staircase do not encounter those going up.

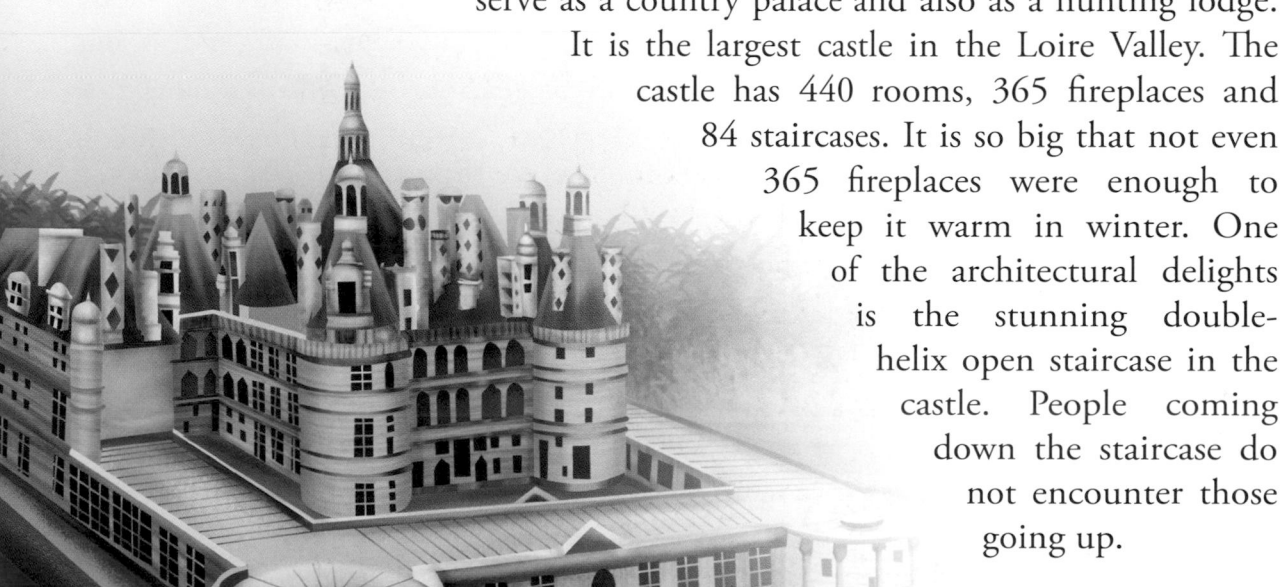

10 SOLOMON R. GUGGENHEIM MUSEUM

The Solomon R. Guggenheim Museum is located in New York City, United States. The Guggenheim Museum was designed by Frank Lloyd Wright. The museum was opened on October 21, 1959. It is shaped roughly like a teacup. The building houses paintings by Brancusi, Braque, Calder, Chagall, Delaunay, Giacometti, Kandinsky, Klee, Leger, Miro, Picasso and Van Gogh.

11 BERCHTESGADEN

Berchtesgaden is in Germany. It is surrounded by snow-capped peaks. Its streets are narrow and winding. It is a region of spectacular natural beauty with majestic mountains and crystal clear lakes. Some famous sights are Lake Koenigsee, Jenner Mountain, Hitler's Eagle's Nest and Salt Mines. It is also a haven for hikers. In Berchtesgaden, tourism is the main source of income.

12 SANTORINI

Santorini is a volcanic island. It is located in the Aegean Sea, about 200 kilometres from Greece's mainland. It is the remains of a volcanic explosion. It has a giant central lagoon. Measuring about 12 kilometres by 7 kilometres, it is surrounded by 300-metre high steep cliffs on three sides.

13 MAMMOTH CAVE NATIONAL PARK

Mammoth Cave National Park is in Kentucky, U.S. It is the world's longest cave system. The cave currently measures 350 miles long and 379 feet deep. It is an example of limestone formations. The park was established as a national park in 1941. It became a World Heritage Site in 1981. Wildlife includes white-tailed deer, foxes, opossums, squirrels, rabbits, bats, reptiles and birds. People go canoeing, fishing, hiking and camping as well.

14 NATURAL TUNNEL STATE PARK

The Natural Tunnel State Park is in Virginia. The park opened in 1971. The Natural Tunnel is the main attraction of the park. It is a massive naturally formed cave so large that it is used as a railroad tunnel. The creation of the tunnel began more than a million years ago. The walls of the tunnel show evidence of prehistoric life and many fossils can be found in the creek bed and on the tunnel walls. A railroad was constructed through the natural tunnel in 1893. The facilities offered at the park include a campground, picnic areas, amphitheatre, visitors centre with a gift shop, historical blockhouse, swimming pool and a chair lift to the tunnel floor.

15 HANGING GARDENS OF BABYLON

The Hanging Gardens of Babylon are in Iraq. They are considered to be one of the original Seven Wonders of the Ancient World. They were built by the Babylonian King Nebuchadnezzar II around 600 BC. He is said to have built the gardens to please his homesick wife, Amytis of Media, who longed for the trees and fragrant plants of her homeland, Persia. The gardens were destroyed by several earthquakes after the 2nd century BC.

16 CLIFFS OF MOHER

The Cliffs of Moher are in Ireland. At their highest, the cliffs are 214 metres and range for 8 kilometres over the Atlantic Ocean. The cliffs are home to one of the major colonies of cliff-nesting seabirds in Ireland. The area was designated as a Refuge for Fauna in 1988 and as a Special Protection Area for Birds (SPA) in 1989. From the cliffs, one can see the Aran Islands, Galway Bay, the Twelve Bens, the Maam Turk Mountains in Connemara and Loop Head to the south.

17 AMALFI COAST

Amalfi Coast is in Italy. The Amalfi Coastline is the most gorgeous and stunning coastline in the world. The coastline begins at Sorrento and ends at Salerno. The Amalfi Coast drive offers a splendid view of the small towns, isolated bays and deep gorges. It seems as though the towns and villages are clinging to the cliffs which rise from the shimmering blue sea. The Amalfi Coast was designated a UNESCO World Heritage Site in 1997.

18 HIRANO SHRINE

The Hirano Shrine is in Kyoto, Japan. This shrine is popular for its gardens and trees. The shrine was established in AD 794 by Emperor Kammu. The shrine has been the site of an annual cherry blossom festival since AD 985. It has become the oldest regularly held festival in Kyoto. Each year, the festival begins in the morning with a ceremony at the mausoleum of former Emperor Kazan. In the afternoon, a procession travels from the shrine into the neighbouring area and back. The present buildings of the shrine were constructed in the 17th century.

19 KARMRAVOR CHURCH

Karmravor Church is in Armenia. It goes back to the 7th century. It was built by two priests: Gregory and Manas. It is a very small domed church measuring 19 feet 7 inches by 24 feet 6 inches. The small cross-shaped church was made from large square stone blocks. The round tiled dome is in the centre.

20 MONTE ALBAN

Monte Alban is located in Mexico. It is situated on a mountain 400 metres above the Oaxaca Valley. It is the place of a ruined site of Zapotec and Mixtec cultures. It was founded approximately around 500 BC and flourished until AD 750. During the Mesoamerican period, much of the state of Oaxaca was controlled from here. Its main structures are the Danzantes (Gallery of Dancers), the Great Plaza, System II, Building J, Central Building G.H., the Palace, the Ball Court, the southern platform, System 7 Dccr and Tomb Number 7 of the Great Plaza. The oldest known formation at Monte Alban is the Gallery of the Dancers. The glyphs portray childbirth, dwarfism, captives, the sick or the dead with twisted body positions (like dancers).

21 TAAL VOLCANO

Taal volcano is located in the Philippines. The volcano is part of a chain of volcanoes along the western side of the island of Luzon. It is said to be the smallest active volcano in the world and is about 700 meters high. The volcano has erupted violently several times. Till date around 6000 people have lost their lives because of volcanic eruptions.

22 OLD TOWN FLORENCE

Old Town Florence is in Oregon, U.S. There are 17 lakes and rivers in and around Florence, presenting fishing, kayaking, hiking, etc. There are towering sand dunes around Florence. These dunes rise to 500 feet above sea level. The Sea Lion Caves are another attraction of Florence. Here you will find sea lions. The Dolly Wares Doll museum in Florence houses a wide variety of dolls.

23 ALCAZAR OF SEVILLE

Alcazar of Seville is in Spain. It was constructed in the 12th century during the reign of Almohad. It was again rebuilt in 1364 during the reign of Pedro, the Cruel. It was originally a Moorish fort. It is a beautiful architectural work of art. The Alcazar is one of the finest existing examples of the Mudejar architecture in the country. The rooms, patios and halls differ in architectural styles from the Islamic to Neoclassical. The beautiful gardens and fountains are particularly worth visiting.

24 NA PALI COAST

San Na Pali Coast is a rough coast on the north shore of Kauai, Hawaii. 'Na Pali' means 'cliffs' in Hawaiian. One can see the cliffs soaring upwards along the coast. Some of the activities done here are sailing, rafting and hiking. Movies like *The Thorn Birds* and portions of *South Pacific* have been filmed along this coast. There are numerous sea caves, small beaches and high waterfalls here. The area is often covered by clouds. Dolphins can often be seen swimming around the area during the early morning.

25 PANORAMA ROUTE

The Panorama Route is in Mpumalanga, South Africa. The route is one of the most beautiful and popular travel destinations in South Africa. It winds its way through the northern Drakensberg Mountains and the northeastern part of the Great Escarpment. Some important sights to visit are the Blyde River Canyon Reserve, the waterfalls in Graskop and Sabie and the Echo Caves. The Blyde River Canyon Reserve is home to some of the best wildlife and birdlife. The Blyde River is the world's third-largest and South Africa's largest canyon.

26 SIGIRIYA

Sigiriya is a site in Sri Lanka. It is also known as the Lion's rock. It is an ancient rock fortress and palace ruin. It was created by King Kasyapa who ruled from AD 477 to 495. The whole structure has been ruined except for the paws of the lion that are still visible. The palace is surrounded by the remains of an extensive network of gardens and reservoirs. It was designated a UNESCO World Heritage Site in 1982.

27 MAUSOLEUM OF HALICARNASSUS

Halicarnassus is located at Bodrum on the Aegean Sea. The Mausoleum of Halicarnassus dates back to the 4th century. It was one of the ancient Seven Wonders of the World. Queen Artemisia commissioned the Mausoleum at Halicarnassus in 353 BC for her husband. It contains the remains of the ancient King Mausolus of Caria. The burial chamber is decorated with gold and the tomb in the mausoleum is shining white. The mausoleum is 140 feet high and covers an area of about 120 feet by 100 feet. The roof of the mausoleum had a sculpture of four horses pulling a chariot carrying King Mausolus and his Queen Artemisia.

28 NATIONAL GALLERY

The National Gallery is in London. It is an art museum that houses Great Britain's national collection of European paintings. It was made in 1824 when the House of Commons bought a collection of 38 paintings from a banker, John Julius Angerstein. Apart from works of such renowned artists as Monet, Rembrandt and da Vinci, the museum contains more than 2300 paintings created between 1250 and 1900. Van Gogh's famous 'Sunflowers' and John Constable's 'The Hay Wain' are displayed here. Apart from offering courses and lectures, the gallery organises touring exhibitions in cities throughout Britain.

29 JIUZHAIGOU

Jiuzhaigou is in the northern part of Sichuan Province. The valley reaches a height of more than 4800 metres. Jiuzhaigou means 'valley of nine villages,' because it once harboured nine villages. Some 140 bird species can be spotted here, as well as a number of endangered plant and animal species, including the giant panda. Some of the activities that can be pursued here are hiking and horseback. It was declared a UNESCO World Heritage Site in 1992.

30 BONIFACIO

Bonifacio is a town located on the southern tip of the island of Corsica, France. It is a narrow peninsula of dazzling white limestone creating a town site unlike any other. Bonifacio is divided into two parts: upper town and harbour. There are some nice beaches in Bonifacio.

31 MAULBRONN MONASTERY

Maulbronn Monastery is situated on the northern border of Germany. The abbey was built in 1147 by 12 monks. The monastery is surrounded by fortified walls and features an elaborate water management system.

It is one of the best preserved medieval monuments in the world. The monastery was built in the Gothic and Romanesque style. Maulbronn was designated a UNESCO World Heritage Site in 1993.

Did You Know?

- Sea Cucumbers, an expensive Asian delicacy, are found at the Galapagos Islands and are so much in demand that there are quotas for them.
- Lake Baikal is 25 million years old, making it the oldest lake in the world.
- The Red Sea has more than 1,200 species of fish out of which 10 per cent are unique to the Red Sea alone.

1 COLOSSEUM

The Colosseum is an amphitheatre in Rome. Its construction began between AD 70 and 72 during the rule of Vespasian. Titus dedicated it officially in AD 80 in a ceremony which included 100 days of games. The Colosseum measures 620 feet by 513 feet (190 m by 155 m). It was almost exactly like a football stadium today. It was built of concrete, marble and limestone. It was capable of seating 50,000 spectators. It was originally known as the Flavian amphitheatre. It is the largest amphitheatre to have ever been built in the Roman Empire and was oval shaped. Though the colosseum was broken by natural disasters like earthquake, it is still one of the favourite places of tourists. The Colosseum was a place where a lot of people could sit and watch entertainment. The entertainment was mostly people killing animals, or people killing each other.

There were 80 entrances, two being reserved for the emperor and his staff. The central area, the arena, was covered with a wooden floor and canvas to make it waterproof. Over this was a layer of sand to absorb blood. The arena was surrounded by a 5-metre-high wall to protect spectators from attacks by wild beasts. At the top of the wall was the podium, on which the royals and others important people had their seats. Above this was the cavea or seating area. This was divided into three parts: the lowest for the knights, the middle for wealthy citizens and the top for the general population.

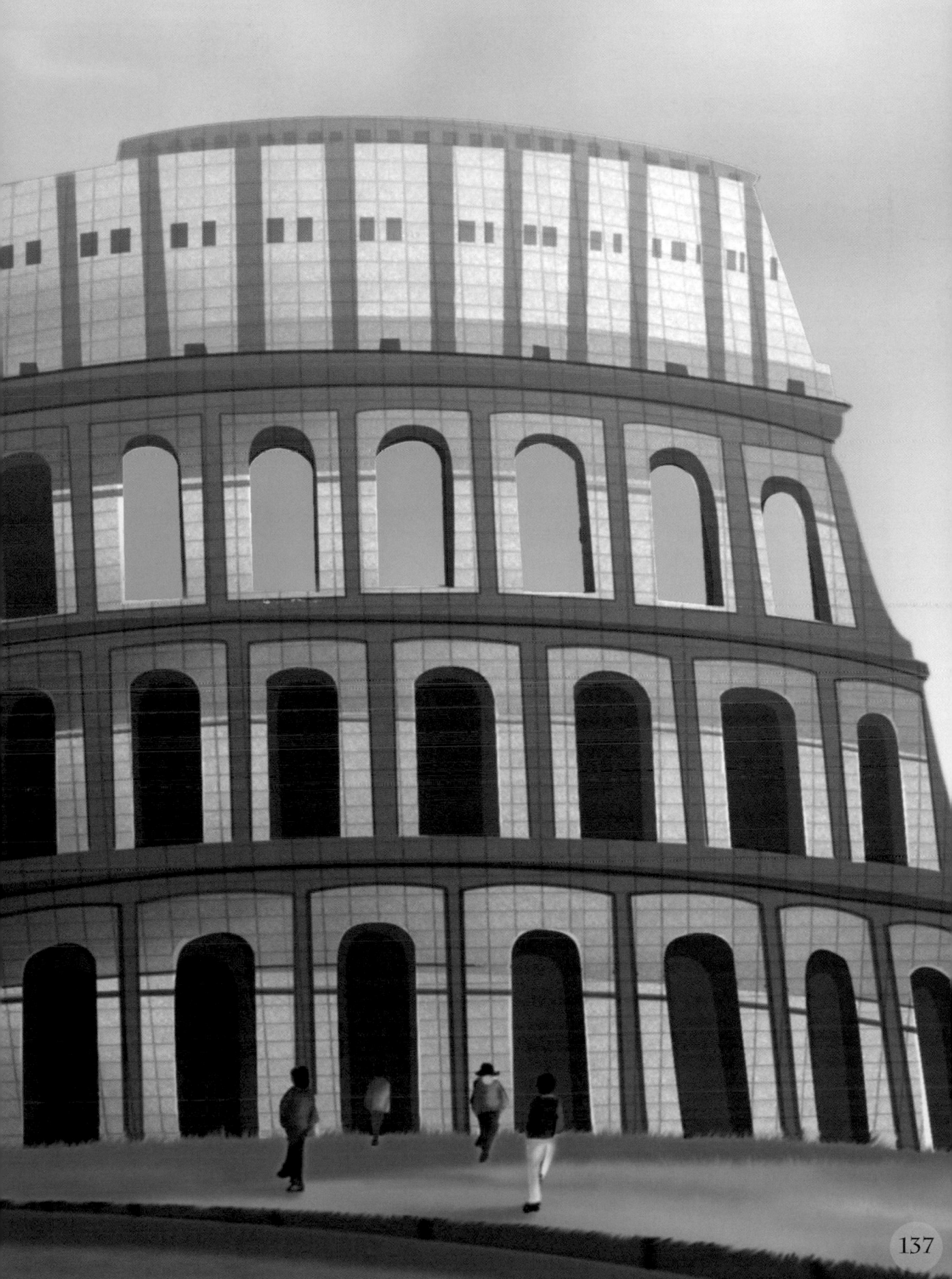

2 EVERGLADES

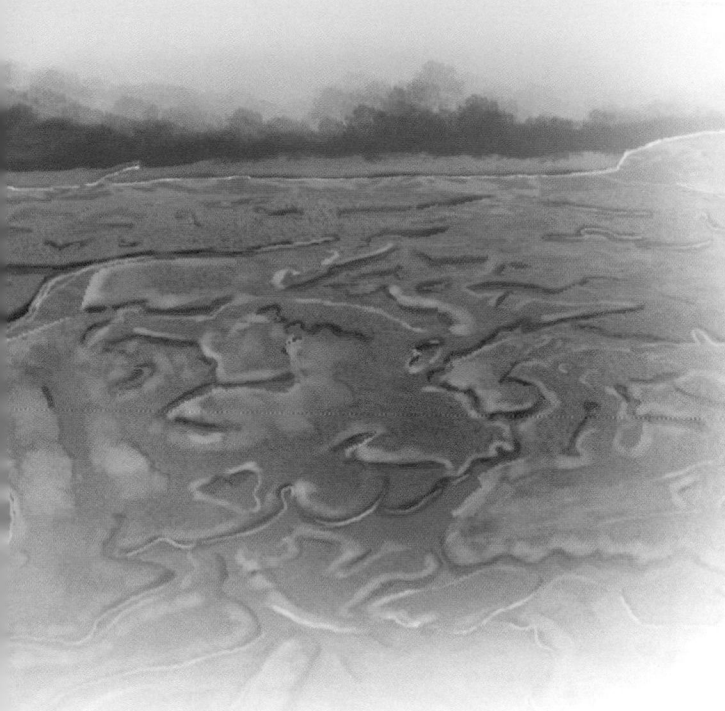

The Everglades are subtropical wetlands in southern Florida. They are popularly called 'River of Grass' to describe the sawgrass marshes. The water forms a slow-moving river 60 miles wide and over 100 miles long, flowing southward to Florida Bay. The everglades experience regular flooding in the wet season and drought in the dry season. Glade refers to an open, grassy area in the forest or a moist, swampy area.

3 SERA MONASTERY

The Sera Monastery is in Lhasa, Tibet. It is at the foot of Tatipu Hill. It is one of the three famous monasteries in Lhasa. The Sera Monastery is dedicated to the Gelugpa or Yellow Hat Sect which is a branch of Tibetan Buddhism, founded by Tsongkhapa. Jamchen Chojey, one of Tsongkhapa's disciples built the monastery in 1419. The word 'Sera' means wild rose in Tibetan language, because the hill behind it was covered with wild roses when the monastery was built. The monastery covers an area of 1,14,946 square metres (28 acres). Its main buildings are the Coqen Hall, Zhacang (college) and Kamcun (dormitory). Scriptures written in gold powder, fine statues, scent cloth and unparalleled murals can be found in these halls.

4 TOWER BRIDGE

The Tower Bridge is over the Thames River in London, England. It was designed by Sir Horace Jones and was completed in 1894. The length of the bridge is 60 metres and its towers can rise to a height of 43 metres. It is made of 11,000 tons of steel and is covered with Cornish granite and Portland stone which give it a fashionable Gothic look. It is one of London's best-known landmarks.

5 CANADIAN ROCKIES

The Canadian Rockies are a part of the Rocky Mountain range extending to Canada. The Canadian Rockies have several high peaks and ranges, such as Mount Robson (3954 m) and Mount Columbia (3747 m). The Canadian Rockies are composed of shale and limestone. They include a huge number of smaller mountain ranges, each with its characteristic landscape, moisture, plant and animal life. Wildlife includes wildlife including bears, elk and eagles. Visitors enjoy the majestic snow-capped peaks, plunging waterfalls, gushing brooks, lakes, lavish meadows and pine-scented mountain air.

6 SEVILLE CATHEDRAL

The Cathedral of Seville is in Spain. The Seville Cathedral was built over a grand mosque. It was built during the 15th and 16th centuries in Gothic style. It is the largest place of worship in Spain. Seville Cathedral was designated a UNESCO World Heritage Site in 1987. The total area of the cathedral is 11,520 square metres. The Cathedral also has a large collection of religious jewellery, paintings and sculptures. Christopher Columbus is also buried here.

7 VAVA'U

Vava'u island group is in Tonga in the southwestern Pacific Ocean. Its climate is suitable for swimming, snorkelling, diving and yachting. It is an excellent place for whale watching because they migrate in large numbers from Antarctica to Vava'u to give birth and rear their offspring in the area's sheltered waters. The waters around Vava'u are occupied by plenty of marine life including over 100 species of colourful tropical fish.

8 KASHMIR

Kashmir is in India. It is a beautiful and popular tourist destination. It is known for its breathtaking scenic beauty. The Dal Lake is a very popular tourist spot in Kashmir. It is surrounded by snow-capped mountain peaks. Kashmir is also known for its romantic Mogul Gardens. Another remarkable feature is the floating vegetable and flower markets. The houseboats or *shikaras* in the Dal Lake are popular with the tourists visiting Kashmir. There are orchards of almonds, apples, apricots, peaches, pears and walnuts. Saffron is also produced here. Buffalo, cattle, sheep goats and poultry are among the livestock that are raised. Silk weaving, shawls (especially *pashmina*), woodcarving, brassware and carpet weaving are some of the major industries.

9 CAPE TOWN

Cape Town is in South Africa. It is the largest and second most populous city in South Africa. It is the oldest city in the country and has a cultural heritage spanning more than 300 years. Some of the places to see are the Table Mountain, Victoria and Alfred Waterfront and Robben Island.

10 TAXCO

Taxco is in Mexico. It is well known for its silver products. This city has cobblestone streets, colonial buildings and white houses with red tiled roofs. The other attraction is the *Catedral de Santa Prisca* (Santa Prisca Cathedral). The cathedral is one of the most fascinating structures that represents baroque architecture. The Silver Museum has silver objects, such as earrings, necklaces, bracelets and other items that have incredible designs.

11 PUERTO PRINCESA SUBTERRANEAN RIVER NATIONAL PARK

The Puerto Princesa Subterranean River National Park is in Philippines. The main feature of the park is a limestone karst mountain landscape with an underground river. The underground river winds through a spectacular cave before emptying into the South China Sea. It is considered to be the world's longest underground river. The river has major formations of stalactites and stalagmites, with several large chambers. The park has a cave that overlooks a clear lagoon bordered with ancient trees around the rim. The beach near the cave is frequented by monkeys, monitor lizards and squirrels. The park has been designated a UNESCO World Heritage Site in 1972.

12 ORVIETO

Orvieto is in Umbria, Italy. The town sits grandly on a large piece of volcanic tuff. One of the attractions of Orvieto is the Duomo, a cathedral. It is known for its portico that is clad with mosaics, statues, and stained glass. Further there is the San Brizio Chapel which has frescoes. St. Patrick's Well is another attraction. Other attractions include a pre-Roman Etruscan necropolis and the Etruscan museum. Orvieto is famous for its ceramics as well.

13 NEWGRANGE

Newgrange is in Ireland. It was built around 3000 BC. It is one of finest European passage-tombs built atop a small hillock. This site was basically designed to document the winter solstice. Newgrange is approximately 80 metres (250 ft) wide and 12 metres (40 ft) high. The arched roof of the central chamber is 6 metres (20 ft) high and the narrow inner passage leading to it is 18 metres (60 ft) long. Newgrange has some stunning examples of megalithic art. It was designated a UNESCO World Heritage Site in 1993.

14 DIONYSUS THEATRE

The Dionysus Theatre was in Athens, Greece. It was major open-air theatre. The theatre was dedicated to Dionysus, the God of plays and wine. The works of ancient Greek playwrights like Aeschylus, Aristophanes, Euripides and Sophocles were premiered here. It was the world's first theatre built of stone. Around 15,000 to 17,000 spectators could sit in the theatre.

15 CHATEÂU DE CHENONCEAU

Chateâu de Chenonceau is in the Loire Valley, France. It is one of the most beautiful chateaus of the Loire Valley. The chateau is also known as the 'Chateau of the Ladies' because it was owned and improved by a several women of royalty, including Queen Catherine de Medici. Chenonceau is known for its architecture and for its collection of art and Renaissance furniture. It also has a large collection of masterpieces by Le Primatice, Rubens and Le Tintoret. It has gardens that are traditional French style with plenty of small, meticulously shaped shrubs. The garden's floral decoration changes in the spring.

16 GANDEN MONASTERY

The Ganden Monastery is in Tibet. It was built in 1409 by the Buddhist leader Tsongkhapa Ganden means 'paradise' in the Tibetan language. The main assembly hall is the main attraction of the monastery. Over a hundred columns support the room. It is large enough to house several thousand chanting monks. Other places to see include the tomb of Tsongkhapa and the Ngam Cho Khang chapel. The monastery also has a number of famous murals and sculptures.

17 PALACE OF VERSAILLES

The Palace of Versailles is in Versailles, France. In French, it is known as the *Château de Versailles*. Initially, it was a hunting lodge for Louis XIII (reigned 1610–43) and his family. But under Louis XIV (1643–1715), it was changed into an extravagant palace surrounded by gardens. In 1682 it became the seat of the French government. One of the most famous rooms in the palace is the Hall of Mirrors. The room is named so because light from 17 windows on one side of the room is reflected by the corresponding arched mirrors on the opposite wall. There are lovely pieces of art and chandeliers in the hall as well.

18 SUMMER PALACE

The Summer Palace is in Beijing, China. Its Chinese name, Yiheyan, translates as Garden for Maintaining Health and Harmony. It is one of the largest imperial gardens in the world. There are various things to see here. Some of them are the Marble Boat and the Long Corridor. The Marble Boat is not made of marble but of stone painted to look like marble. The ceilings and the columns of the Long Hall are painted with different landscapes and animal scenes. Some other attractions are Seventeen Arch Bridge, Hall of Benevolence and Longevity and a boat ride on the Kunming Lake.

19 RIQUEWIHR

Riquewihr is in Alsace, France. It is known for its historical architecture. The place is known for its vineyards. Some great wines are produced here. Riquewihr looks the same as it did in the 16th century. One can see well-preserved medieval houses and shops here.

20 DEUTSCHES MUSEUM

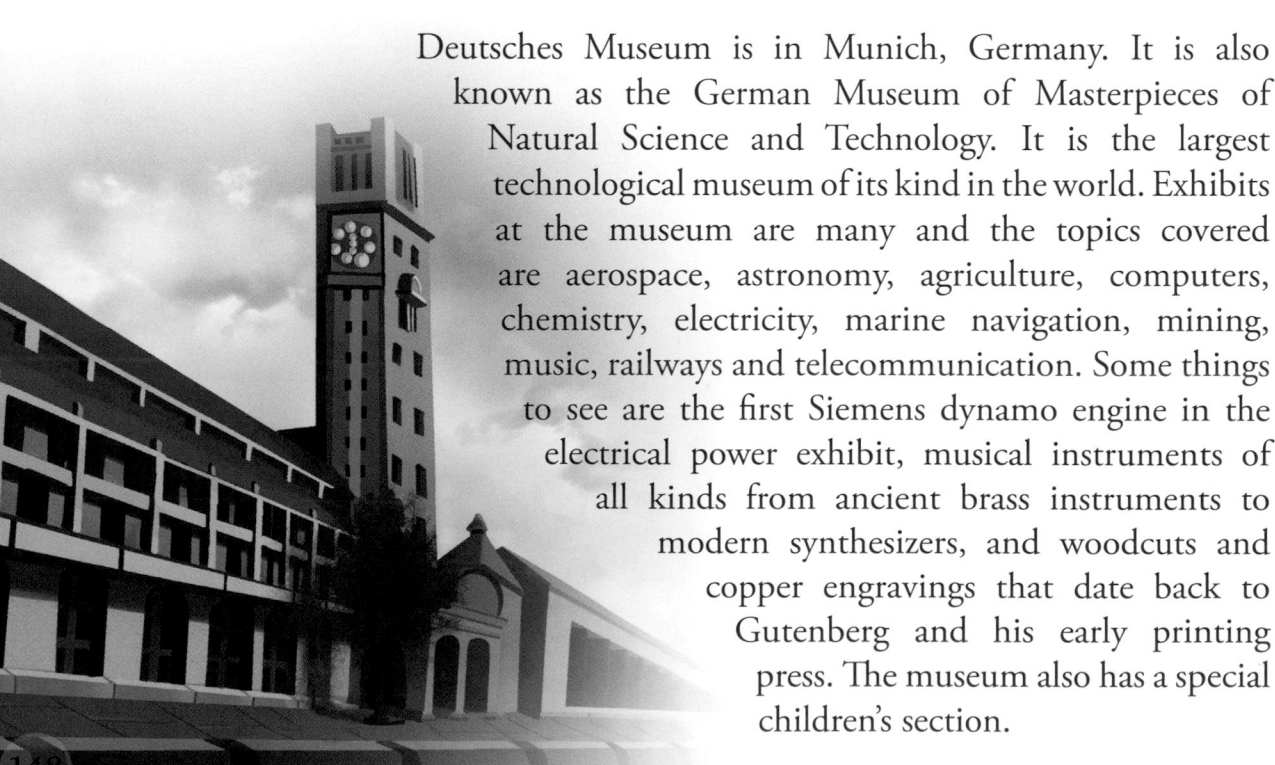

Deutsches Museum is in Munich, Germany. It is also known as the German Museum of Masterpieces of Natural Science and Technology. It is the largest technological museum of its kind in the world. Exhibits at the museum are many and the topics covered are aerospace, astronomy, agriculture, computers, chemistry, electricity, marine navigation, mining, music, railways and telecommunication. Some things to see are the first Siemens dynamo engine in the electrical power exhibit, musical instruments of all kinds from ancient brass instruments to modern synthesizers, and woodcuts and copper engravings that date back to Gutenberg and his early printing press. The museum also has a special children's section.

21 EPIDAURUS

Epidaurus theatre is in Greece. The theatre was built around the 4th century BC. It was abandoned about a thousand years later. It lay buried until excavations began in 1881. At present, an annual festival takes place in the theatre every year from July-August (on Fridays and Satrudays). It is one of the top theatre events in Greece. Dramas by Aristophanes, Euripides, Sophocles and other illustrious ancient Greek playwrights are performed.

22 GOMATESHWARA

The Gomateshwara statue is in Sravanabelagola, Karnataka, India. The statue is 17 metres high and stands majestically on top of a hill. The statue was built around AD 983 by Chamundraya, a minister of the Ganga King, Rajamalla. A single large stone was used in the construction of the Gomateshwara Statue. It is the tallest monolithic statue in the world. The statue depicts Lord Gomateshwara, a Jain saint. Every 12 years, devotees celebrate the Mahamastakabhisheka festival. During the festival, the statue of Lord Gomateswara is bathed in milk, curd, ghee (clarified butter), saffron and gold coins.

23 SKELLIG MICHAEL

Skellig Michael is in Ireland. It is a small, rocky island rising out of the Atlantic Ocean. Irish monks occupied it from the 6th to 12th century. The monastery was small and could accommodate only a few monks. The monks lived in beehive-shaped stone huts built without mortar. Despite being old, they have been well preserved. The monastery was designated a UNESCO World Heritage Site in 1996.

24 SAN MIGUEL DE ALLENDE

San Miguel de Allende is located in central Mexico. It was founded in 1542 by the Franciscan monk Juan de San Miguel. The central part is known for its churches and various colonial buildings and is a national historical monument. The town is the centre for art, music, cooking and language schools. One of the main attractions is the pink-toned La Parroquia (Parish Church) on the main plaza. The city also hosts world-famous events such as the Chamber Music Festival and the San Miguel Jazz Festival, which features renowned artists.

25 PHINDA PRIVATE GAME RESERVE

Phinda Private Game Reserve is situated in the KwaZulu-Natal region in northern South Africa. It comprises 23,000 hectares (56,800 acres) of prime conservation land. Phinda Private Game Reserve is home to a variety of mammals. One can find the lion, leopard, elephant, rhino and buffalo. The habitat also houses over 380 bird species.

26 ALCATRAZ ISLAND

The Alcatraz Island is located in San Francisco, California. Before 1972, the island served as a lighthouse, a military fortification and a prison. It was nicknamed the Rock. In 1972, Alcatraz became a national recreation area. The island offers a close look at the historic prison. The island is also a wildlife sanctuary with birds, and tide pools filled with crabs. Western gull and black-crowned heron colonies are prevalent in the area. More than a million tourists visit Alcatraz annually.

27 PLAZA MAYOR

The Plaza Mayor is a grand square in the centre of Madrid, Spain. The original building was built between 1617 and 1619. The plaza is completely enclosed by buildings. The oldest and most famous building is the Casa del Panaderia, the bakery house. The Plaza Mayor has been the centre of festivities like bull fights, royal coronations and executions. At the centre of the square is a bronze statue of King Philips III.

28 RIO DE JANEIRO

The Rio de Janeiro is in Brazil. The city cuddles between the green mountains and the blue Guanabara Bay. Corcovado Mountain and Sugar Loaf are the two major attractions of the city. The top of the Corcovado Mountain is its most popular viewpoint. The mountain is 710 metres high. Sugar Loaf Peak is 400 metres high.

29 MOUNT TAISHAN

Mount Taishan is in the Shandong province, China. Taishan means '*Mount Tai*' (the Chinese word 'shan' means mountain). It is known as the 'First of the Five Sacred Mountains'. In ancient times, the emperors used to climb Mount Taishan and pray to heaven and earth or their ancestors. Stone carvings at Mount Taishan include the Buddhist Diamond Sutra in Jing Shi Valley, the Scripture of Mt. Tai and the Mo Ya Tablet. Besides historic relics, Mount Taishan boasts of unique natural scenery too. Mount Taishan was designated a UNESCO World Heritage Site in 1987.

30 LATIN QUARTER

The Latin Quarter is located on the bank of the Seine River, France. It is a major tourist attraction in Paris. The area is generally associated with artists, intellectuals, and a bohemian way of life. The place has many monuments, museums and gardens. Some of them are the Institut du Monde Arabe, Musée de Cluny or the Muséum National d'Histoire Naturelle.

31 GARMISCH-PARTENKIRCHEN

Garmisch-Partenkirchen is in Bavaria, Germany. It is an international winter resort and a regional commercial centre. Garmisch-Partenkirchen was founded by uniting the two towns of Garmisch and Partenkirchen by a decree of Adolf Hitler to bring the 1936 Winter Olympics to Germany. During summer, people can go for a hike or do bicycling or mountain climbing.

Did You Know?

- The Serengeti ecosystem is home to 70 large mammal species and 500 avifauna species.
- In 1964-1966, there were 108 rhinos in the Ngorongoro Conservation Area. In 1995, only 11-14 were recorded.

1 CHRIST THE REDEEMER

Christ the Redeemer is a statue of Jesus Christ in Rio de Janeiro, Brazil. The statue is 120 feet tall and weighs 635 tones. It is made of concrete and soapstone. The statue is located at the summit of Corcovado Mountain in Tijuca Forest National Park standing and looking over the city. As a vantage point, it offers superb views of Rio de Janeiro, the bay, Sugarloaf Mountain and Copacabana and Ipanema Beaches. It is a symbol of Christianity and is an important icon of Brazil. There is a chapel for 150 people at the base of the statue. It was designed by Heitor da Silva Costa and created by sculptor Paul Landowski. The statue took five years to construct. The construction was completed in 1931. It has become a symbol of the city and of the warmth of the Brazilian people, who receive visitors with open arms. It is now a part of the new Seven Wonders of the World.

2 GREAT OCEAN ROAD

The Great Ocean Road is a stretch of road along the southeastern coast of Australia between Torquay and Warrnambool. The drive along this stretch offers beautiful sceneries, amazing wildlife, cascading waterfalls, incredible beaches, and more. The road was built by returning soldiers between 1919 and 1932. It is the largest war memorial in the world and is dedicated to the casualties of World War I.

3 BUNGLE BUNGLE

Bungle Bungle is a part of the Purnululu National Park, Australia. It has beehive-shaped sandstone domes that soar up to hundreds of feet. The mounds have alternate horizontal striped bands of orange, gray and black. There are Aborigine rock paintings and burial grounds in Bungle Bungle as well. Despite being made of soft sandstone the range has survived for more than 350 million years. The mounds appear hard but are delicate and can crumble easily.

4 GANGKHAR PUENSUM

Gangkhar Puensum is the highest mountain in Bhutan. It is the highest unclimbed mountain in the world. After Bhutan was opened for mountaineering in 1983, there were four expeditions that made failed summit attempts in 1985 and 1986. However, in 1998, a team successfully climbed a subsidiary peak of the mountain from Tibet. The peak of Gangkhar Puensum has never been summited.

5 OLD QUEBEC CITY

Old Quebec City is the capital of the Canadian province of Quebec. The city is divided into two sections: Upper Town and Lower Town. The Upper Town has the famous castle-inspired Chateau Frontenac hotel, the icon of Quebec. The streets are lined with old buildings. The Lower Town has the look of a traditional Quebec. A winter carnival is held in Quebec which goes on for 17 days. The Old Town was designated a UNESCO World Heritage Site in 1985.

6 HANGING MONASTERY

The Hanging Monastery is in Datong, China. It was built in AD 491. The Chinese name of the Hanging Monastery is Xuankong. The monastery is also known as the Hengshan Hanging Monastery. The pavilions of the monastery cling to the cliff and seem to be hanging. The pavilions are built almost fully of wood. The monks expanded the pavilions by digging caves in the cliff behind them. These caves contain religious statues. One cave has the statues of Buddha, Confucius and Laotsu sitting side by side.

7 SOUTH POLE

The South Pole is on the continent of Antarctica. It is also known as the Geographic South Pole or Terrestrial South Pole. It is the southernmost point on the surface of the Earth. The ice is estimated to be about 9000 feet thick at the pole. Due to its exceptionally harsh climate, there are no native resident plants or animals at the South Pole. During the southern winter, the South Pole receives no sunlight at all, and from May to July, between extended periods of twilight, it is completely dark.

8 LE PUY-EN-VELAY

Le Puy-en-Velay is in France. It is a major pilgrimage town. A red cast-iron statue (53 ft high) of Our Lady of France was erected in 1860 on a hill. At the foot of the hill stands the 11th–12th-century Romanesque Cathedral of Notre-Dame. Le Puy-en-Velay is the starting point of the 1600-kilometre (1000 mile) walking pilgrimage to Santiago de Compostela in Spain. Handmade lace is a popular product here. Industrial activities include food processing and the manufacture of machinery, plastics, rubber, paper and packaging and textiles.

9 TEMPLE OF HEPHAESTUS

The Temple of Hephaestus is in Athens, Greece. The temple dates back to the 5th century BC. It is dedicated to the God Hephaestus. It was designed by Ictinus. The temple's columns and pediments are intact and so is the roof. Its friezes and other decorations, however, have been badly damaged by thieves and looters over the centuries.

10 HAMPI

Hampi is a village located in northern Karnataka state in India. The site was the last capital of the Hindu Kingdom of Vijayanagar. There are more than 500 monuments here. Among them are beautiful temples, basement of palaces, remains of aquatic structures, ancient market streets, royal pavilions, bastions, royal platforms, treasury buildings, etc. The site is significant historically and architecturally. It was designated a UNESCO World Heritage Site in 1986.

11 BLARNEY STONE

The Blarney Stone is a block of bluestone built into the fortifications of Blarney Castle, Blarney, Ireland. The stone was set into a tower of the castle in 1446. More than 3,00,000 people come to kiss the Blarney Stone each year, in the hopes of gaining a more expressive speech. The word 'blarney' means clever, flattering, or coaxing talk.

12 BARGELLO MUSEUM

Bargello Museum is in Florence, Italy. It was a former barrack and prison that was converted into an art museum. It was first opened in 1865. This museum houses a superb collection of 13th to 16th-century sculptures. It displays the largest Italian collection of Gothic and Renaissance sculptures, including masterpieces of Luca della Robbia, Verrocchio, Donatello, Michelangelo and Cellini. The museum also has a fine collection of ceramics, textile, tapestries, armours and old coins. It is one of the city's oldest public buildings.

13 KIMBERLEY DIAMOND MINE

Kimberley Diamond Mine also known as the Big Hole is in South Africa. The diamond mine holds the title of being the largest hand-dug hole in the world. From 1866 to 1914 50,000 miners dug the hole with picks and shovels, yielding 2722 kilos of diamonds. The Big Hole has a surface of 17 hectares (42 acres) and is 463 metres wide. The Kimberly Diamond Mine is the core of an ancient volcano. The extreme heat and pressure of volcanism produced the diamonds out of carbon-rich rocks.

14 SMITHSONIAN INSTITUTION

The Smithsonian Institution is in the United States of America. It is one of the largest museum complexes in the world. It has 18 major museums, a national zoo and a number of research centres. About 20 million visitors visit the institute annually. The complex includes the National Air and Space Museum; National Museum of Natural History; the Smithsonian world-class art museums which includes Cooper-Hewitt National Design Museum, Freer Gallery of Art, Hirshorn Museum and Sculpture Garden, National Museum of American History, National Museum of the American Indian and Natural Portrait Gallery; and National Zoological Park. The institution belongs to and is run by the U.S. Government.

15 BUND

The Bund is an area of Huangpu district in China. The Bund derives its name from an Anglo-Indian word for a flood preventing embankment. It is 1500 metres in length. Once, the Bund was known as the financial capital of Asia. But, after the worldwide stock market crash of 1929, it began to lose that position. It is the world's most famous riverside street. The Bund has dozens of historical buildings lining the Huangpu River. One can also catch a grand view of the Pudong modern skyscrapers across the river.

16 LADAKH

Ladakh is in Jammu and Kashmir, India. It is called the Land of the High Passes. It lies between the Himalayan and the Karakorum ranges. The most attractive feature of Ladakh is the Buddhist monasteries. Besides the monasteries, the 9-story Leh Palace, Stok Palace Museum and the Central Institute of Buddhist Studies at Choglamsar, Mosque and Moravian Church are added attraction for the tourists.

17 YANGTZE RIVER CRUISE

The Yangtze River is the largest river of China. During the cruise, one can see the Three Gorges and the Three Gorges Dam. The cruise runs between Chongqing and Yichang. The length is 660 kilometres (410 miles). The three spectacular river gorges are the Qutang Gorge, the Wu Gorge and the Xiling Gorge.

18 MILLAU VIADUCT

The Millau Viaduct is a bridge in southern France. It is the tallest bridge in the world at 343 metres. It was designed by Michel Virlogeux and British architect Norman Foster. This four-lane bridge opened in 2005 and can accommodate 25,000 vehicles per day. It has a steel deck, rather than the more usual concrete roadbed. The aim to construct the bridge was to cut the travelling time to southern France.

19 ARAN ISLANDS

The Aran Islands are located at the mouth of Galway Bay on the west coast of Ireland. These are three limestone islands—Inishmore, Inishmaan and Inisheer. The largest island is Inishmore. It is called the 'big island' in Gaelic and is the most populated and the most visited of all the three islands.

The top attraction of Inishmore is Don Aengues, a 2000-year-old fort designed with concentric semi-circular stone walls. It sits boldly on the edge of a 100-metre (330 feet) cliff. Inishmaan is called the 'middle island' and Inisheer, the 'castle island'. The O'Brien's Castle is located in Inisheer, hence the name. These two islands are smaller, much less populated, and have lesser tourists.

20 BORGHESE GALLERY

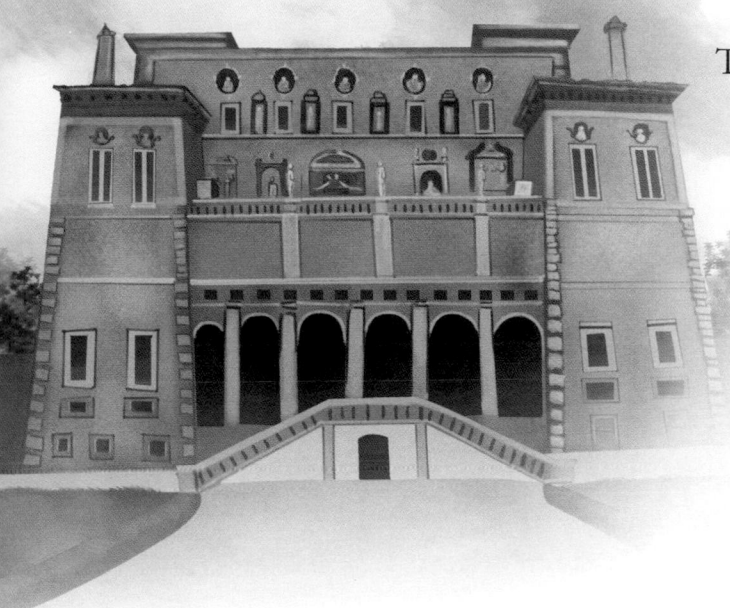

The Borghese Gallery is an art gallery in Rome, Italy. The gallery is one of the world's best small art museums and is famous for Italian Baroque paintings and ancient sculptures. The collection was started by Cardinal Scipione Borghese in the early 1600s. There is a wide collection of early marble statues of Bernini. The most famous artworks of the museum are Apollo and Daphne and Pauline Borghese.

21 MEZQUITA

Mezquita is a cathedral located in Cordoba, Spain. The site of Mezquita originally bore a church. Then the Moors conquered Cordoba in the 8th century. They demolished the church and built a mosque. 'Mezquita' means mosque in Spanish. Five centuries later, the Christians again took over the site. The vast majority of the Mezquita's art and architecture is the work of Islamic architects, who built it as a mosque in the 8th century. One can see a whiff of Persian, Mid Eastern Islamic, Roman and Gothic styles in the architecture of Mezquita.

22 CARTHAGE

Carthage is an ancient city on the Gulf of Tunis. It was founded in 814 BC by the Phoenicians of Tyre. A few things to see are the Roman amphitheatre and the thermal Antonine Baths, once the largest baths built by the Romans. The Byrsa Hill provides a grand view of Carthage. The Byrsa Hill also houses the Carthage Museum. The mosaics, sculptures and artifacts from the period before Carthage was destroyed by Rome in 146 BC. St. Louis Cathedral is also on the hill. It was built by the French in 1890 and is now used for concerts.

23 YOSEMITE NATIONAL PARK

The Yosemite National Park is in California, U.S. The park is known for its spectacular granite cliffs, waterfalls, clear streams and Giant Sequoia groves. Some major attractions of the park are the Half Dome, El Capitan, Bridalveil Falls, Yosemite Falls and Mariposa Grove. The grove is home of the Giant Sequoias. The Saddlebag Lake in Yosemite is the highest lake in the magnificent Eastern Sierra Nevada Mountains.

24 KAKADU NATIONAL PARK

Kakadu National Park is in Australia. It covers an area of nearly 20,000 square kilometres. Some famous attractions are saltwater crocodiles, aboriginal rock paintings and Yellow Water Billabong. It was designated a UNESCO World Heritage Site in 1981. The cave paintings, rock carvings and archaeological sites record the skills and way of life of the regions' inhabitants, from being hunter-gatherers to the present day.

25 JIAYUGUAN FORT

The Jiayuguan Fort is located in China. The fort was built in 1372 during the period of the Ming Dynasty. It was enlarged in 1539. It effectively protected the strategic Jiayuguan Pass for centuries. The fort wall is 10 metres (33 feet) high and very thick. Due to its firm construction and intelligent military layout, the fort was called 'the strongest pass under heaven'. Its outer wall is 733 metres in circumference. Its two gate watchtowers each are 20 metres tall.

26 SAN VITALE BASILICA

San Vitale Basilica is in Ravenna, Italy. It was built in the 6th century. Its construction was started by Ecclesius, the Bishop of Ravenna. The basilica is famous for the finest Byzantine mosaics in Europe. Two of the main mosaics notably feature the Byzantium Emperor Justinian and his wife Theodora. A Greek banker, Iulianus Argentarius sponsored the construction of the basilica. The cost of construction was about 26,000 gold pieces.

27 ARC DE TRIOMPHE

The Arc de Triomphe is a monument in Paris, France. It is the largest triumphal arch in the world. It stands in the centre of the Place Charles de Gaulle. The arch is 164 feet (50 metres) high and 148 feet (45 metres) wide. It was begun by Napoleon Bonaparte and was designed by Jean-François-Thérèse Chalgrin. The construction began in 1806. On the inside, and the top of the arc are the names of all the generals and the wars fought by them.

28 CORFU

Corfu is a Greek island in the Ionian Sea. It is the second largest of the Ionian Islands. An interesting feature of the island is Corfu Old Town. The buildings have Greek, Byzantine, Venetian and French styles. Other interesting features are the mountain valleys and the coast. The land is covered with olive groves. Due to sufficient rains, the land is full of greenery and colourful flowers.

29 RING OF KERRY

The Ring of Kerry is Ireland's most beautiful and scenic drives. One can view rocky coastlines and green hills with sheep on the way. Other things to see are the Lakes of Killarney, Muckross House, Ross Castle and the Staigue Fort. The route is more or less 200 kilometres (125 miles) long. One can go golfing, cycling, walking, riding and fishing out here.

30 MITLA

Mitla is an archaeological site in Oaxaca, Mexico. The Mitla ruins date back to AD 200. The site was built during the Zapotec civilisation. Mitla was a major religious centre. There are five major groups of ruins. At present, only two of them remain. The Columns Group is the best preserved. The House of Pezelao is its major attraction.

Did You Know?

- The Channel Tunnel in United Kingdom is popularly called the 'chunnel'.
- On June 26, 1986, at the ten-year anniversary of the tower, Dan Goodwin used his hands and feet to climb the outside of the CN Tower right to the top, twice.
- The Golden Gate Bridge had the longest suspension bridge span in the world when it was completed in 1937.

1 EIFFEL TOWER

The Eiffel Tower is in Paris, France. Built in 1889, it is the tallest building in Paris. It was designed by engineer Gustave Eiffel and so, it is named after him. The tower is 300 metres (984 ft) high. It rests on a base that is 5 metres (17 ft) high, and a television antenna atop the tower gives it a total elevation of 322 metres (1056 ft). The Eiffel Tower was the world's tallest man-made structure until the construction of the Chrysler Building in Manhattan. The tower is a hugely popular tourist destination. It is one of the most recognisable structures in the world. The tower has two restaurants and both are located on the first floor.

2 LABRANG MONASTERY

The Labrang Monastery is located at the foot of the Phoenix Mountain northwest of Xiahe County in the Gansu Province. The monastery dates back to the year 1709. It is also called the Labuling Monastery. There are six Buddhist colleges in the monastery. There are 60,000 Buddhist sutras and scholarly books in the monastery. The main attraction is the gathering of the monks at the steps of the main hall. They collectively chant as they wait for the prayer building to open its doors.

3 MUSÉE D'ORSAY

Musée d'Orsay is a museum in Paris, France. It mostly has French art dating from 1848 to 1915, including paintings, sculptures, furniture and photographs, and is best known for its wide collection of impressionist masterpieces. There are works by Cezanne, Degas, Gauguin, Manet, Matisse, Monet, Renoir, Seurat, Van Gogh, amongst others. When it opened, the museum contained some 2300 paintings, 1500 sculptures and 1000 other objects.

4 SEQUOIA NATIONAL PARK

The Sequoia National Park is in California, U.S. The park is named after the giant sequoia, the world's largest tree. The Giant Forest is the major attraction of the park.

One can view the General Sherman tree. It is 83 metres (275 feet) high and 31 metres (103 ft) in circumference. Some of the trees are 2000 years old. Other interesting things to see are the Tunnel Log, Crescent Meadow, Moro Rock, Tharp's Log and Crystal Cave.

5 WEST LAKE

West Lake is in Hangzhou, Zhejiang province, China. It is also known as Xi Hú. It is surrounded by mountains on three sides having an area of around 6.5 square kilometres. The circumference is around 15 kilometres. Its average depth is 2.27 metres. The lake has been an inspiration for many poets and writers. The main attraction of West Lake is the Lesser Yingzhou Island.

6 LESHAN GREAT BUDDHA

The statue of Leshan Great Buddha is in Leshan City, Sichuan Province, China. It is the tallest carved statue in the world. It was sculpted out of a hillside more than 1200 years ago. The Buddha is 71 metres (233 ft) high and has 3 metres long (11 ft) fingers. The statue was carved in the 8th century. It depicts a seated Buddha with his hands resting on his knees, gazing across the river.

7 MOUNT ATHOS

Mount Athos is in Greece. It is also called the Holy Mount. There are 20 monasteries spread out on this peninsula. The mount is forbidden to women and children. Only monks live on the mount. It was designated a UNESCO World Heritage Site in 1988. The mount is about 50 kilometres in length, 8 to 12 kilometres in width and covers an area of about 350 square kilometres. The monasteries portray Byzantine style of art.

8 JANTAR MANTAR

Jantar Mantar is in Delhi, India. It was built by Maharaja Jai Singh II of Jaipur in 1724. It is an astronomical observation site. Jantar Mantar means 'instrument for calculation'. The primary purpose of the observatory was to assemble astronomical tables and predict the times and movements of the sun, moon and planets. There are four distinct instruments within the observatory of Jantar Mantar: the Samrat, Ram, Jayaprakash and Mishra yantras.

9 ROCK OF CASHEL

The Rock of Cashel is an archaeological site in Ireland. It sits on a hill 200 feet above the plains. During the early years, this building was used as an assembly place for the kings and then years later it was used by the church. This is why a cathedral and a chapel were built here. Some important ruins are the Round Stone Tower, a Cathedral, a Romanesque Chapel and the Vicar's House.

10 PORTOFINO

Portofino is a small Italian fishing village in Italy. Some famous places to visit are the Statue of Christ, San Giorgio Church and Castello Brown. Castello Brown is a castle that sits on a hill. Other features of Portofino include the array of boats on the bay and villas covered by bougainvilleas.

11 SEGOVIA ALCAZAR

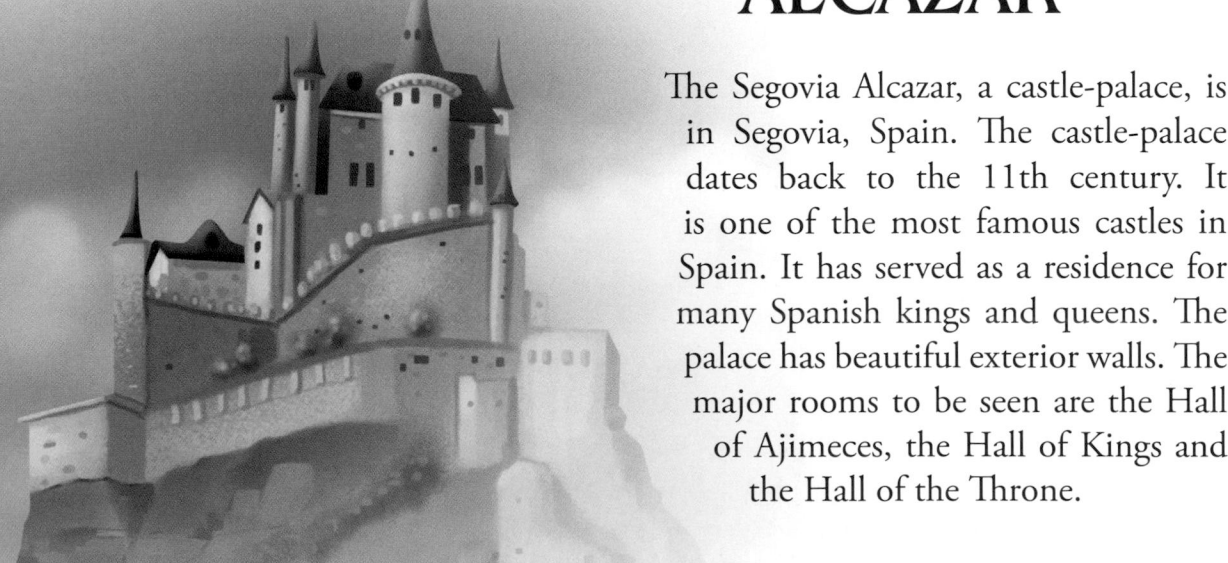

The Segovia Alcazar, a castle-palace, is in Segovia, Spain. The castle-palace dates back to the 11th century. It is one of the most famous castles in Spain. It has served as a residence for many Spanish kings and queens. The palace has beautiful exterior walls. The major rooms to be seen are the Hall of Ajimeces, the Hall of Kings and the Hall of the Throne.

12 BURJ AL ARAB

The Burj Al Arab hotel is in Dubai, United Arab Emirates. Burj Al Arab means '*The Arabian Tower*' in Arabic. Standing at 321 metres on an artificial island, it is the fourth tallest hotel in the world. The structure resembles the sail of a boat. It was designed by Tom Wright and was completed in 1999. The hotel has 202 rooms, 18 elevators and 60 floors. Each suite has its own private butler.

13 BAYOUS

The bayous stretch along the Gulf of Mexico west to east from Houston, Texas to Mobile, Alabama, U.S. The word 'bayou' originated from the term 'bayuk', meaning 'small stream'. A bayou is a water body in a lowland area. The bayous have plenty of wildlife. The main attractions of the bayous are the Swamp Tours and Fishing Charters.

14 LONGMEN CAVES

Longmen Caves are in the Henan province of China. There are some 1350 caves and 40 pagodas with Buddhist statues carved out of the hard limestone cliffs. The carving began in AD 492 and continued for 500 years. Longmen means 'dragon's gate' in Chinese. Ancestor Worshiping Cave is the most famous of all Longmen Caves and is also known as the Fengxian Temple. The caves were designated a UNESCO World Heritage Site in 2000.

15 BERMUDA

Bermuda is on the North Atlantic Ocean. Bermuda is 37 kilometres (23 miles) long and slightly less than 3 kilometres (2 miles) wide at its broadest point. It has beautiful pink sand beaches. People can go snorkelling and diving. The houses are beautifully painted. Bermuda attracts about 200,000 tourists per year.

16 OLD STRASBOURG

Old Strasbourg is in the Alsace region of France. It has well-preserved medieval scenes. There are two main features of Old Strasbourg. First is the Notre Dame Cathedral and the second is the Petite France district. The cathedral is known for its animated astronomical clock. Its spire is 142 metres. The narrow winding streets and half-timbered town houses attract visitors from far and wide.

17 MYCENAE

Mycenae is an archaeological site in Greece. It was once a mighty kingdom of Ancient Greece. The site was first excavated in 1874 by Heinrich Schliemann, a German amateur archaeologist. Homer's famous epic, The Iliad, spins the story of the Trojan War. One key character was Agamemnon, King of Mycenae on the Peloponnesus Peninsula of Greece. One can still see the stone walls, subterranean tombs and the Lion Gate.

18 CAPRI

Capri is an island in the Campania region, Italy. The island is a single block of limestone 3.9 miles (6.25 km) long, with a maximum width of 1.8 miles and an area of 4 square miles (10 square km). Some major attractions of Capri are Blue Grotto, La Piazzetta, Villa Jovis, Farraglioni, Villa San Michelle, Anacapri Vlllage and Marina Grande and Piccola. A large number of migratory birds rest in Capri for many days.

19 SEGOVIA AQUEDUCT

The Segovia Aqueduct is in Segovia, Spain. It carries water 10 miles (16 km) from the Frío River to the city of Segovia, Spain. The structure was built under the Roman emperor Trajan (AD 98–117). It is one of the best-preserved monuments of Roman engineering. It was built with 24,000 dark-coloured Guadarrama granite blocks without the use of mortar. The portion above the ground is 2388 feet (728 m) long and consists of some 165 arches more than 30 feet (9 m) high.

20 EMPIRE STATE BUILDING

The Empire State Building is in New York, U.S. It is a steel-framed 102-story building at a height of 448 metres. It was constructed in 1931. The Empire State Building has featured in many films. It has two observatories. One is on the 86th floor, the other on the 102nd. The top of the Empire State Building is lit up at night in different colours to celebrate various holidays.

21 PINGYAO ANCIENT CITY

The Pingyao ancient city lies in the Shanxi Province of China. The city dates back 2700 years. There are three major attractions: the city wall, streets and old mansions. The city is surrounded by an ancient defensive wall 12 metres high and over 6 kilometres long. Considering its age, the wall is in good condition. Among the museums, the most fascinating is the 19th century Ri Sheng Chang mansion. Though a museum now, it was once the headquarters of one of China's most powerful banks.

22 OPÉRA GARNIER

The Opéra Garnier is in Paris, France and opened in 1875. It was the world's largest theatre and opera house when it opened. Initially, it was known as the Paris Opera House. The first opera performed there was Fromental Halévy's work *La Juive* on January 8, 1875. The building was designed by Charles Garnier and took 14 years to complete. The Opéra Garnier has a total area of 11,000 square metres and a vast stage with room for up to 450 artists. The opera seats 2200 people.

23 KNOSSOS PALACE

Knossos Palace is in Greece. The palace gives an insight into the Minoan civilisation which began around 2000 BC and was probably its governmental, cultural and religious seat. There were over 1300 rooms in the palace. The Knossos Palace was discovered in 1878 by a man named Kalokairinos. Later, in 1900, Sir Evans did a complete excavation job.

24 CINQUE TERRE

The Cinque Terre is in Liguria, Italy. Cinque Terre means '*five lands*' in Italian. The five villages are Monterosso, Vernazza, Manarola, Corniglia and Riomaggiore. The villages hang on the sharp, rocky coastline of Cinque Terre. The Cinque Terre was designated a UNESCO World Heritage Site in 1997. Vernazza and Riomaggiore are the best of the five villages.

25 RONDA

Ronda lies in the Málaga province, Spain. The town is situated on two hills divided by a deep ravine that has the Grande River. Spain's oldest bullring, a stone Neoclassical structure (c. 1785), is also found in Ronda. It is a museum now. Ronda is surrounded by national parks. Los Alcornocales Natural Park is one of them and is Spain's most important cork-oak forests.

26 YELLOWSTONE NATIONAL PARK

The Yellowstone National Park is in the United States and is spread over the states of Wyoming, Idaho and Montana. It is one of the oldest and largest parks. The park was established in 1872 by the U.S. Congress. It was the nation's as well as the world's first national park. Some of the attractions of the park are the Old Faithful Geyser, Mud pools, Grand Canyon, Norris Geyser Basin, Hayden or Lamar Valleys and Mammoth Hot Springs. The park is a protected territory for bears, bison, wolves and elk. The park was designated a UNESCO World Heritage Site in 1978.

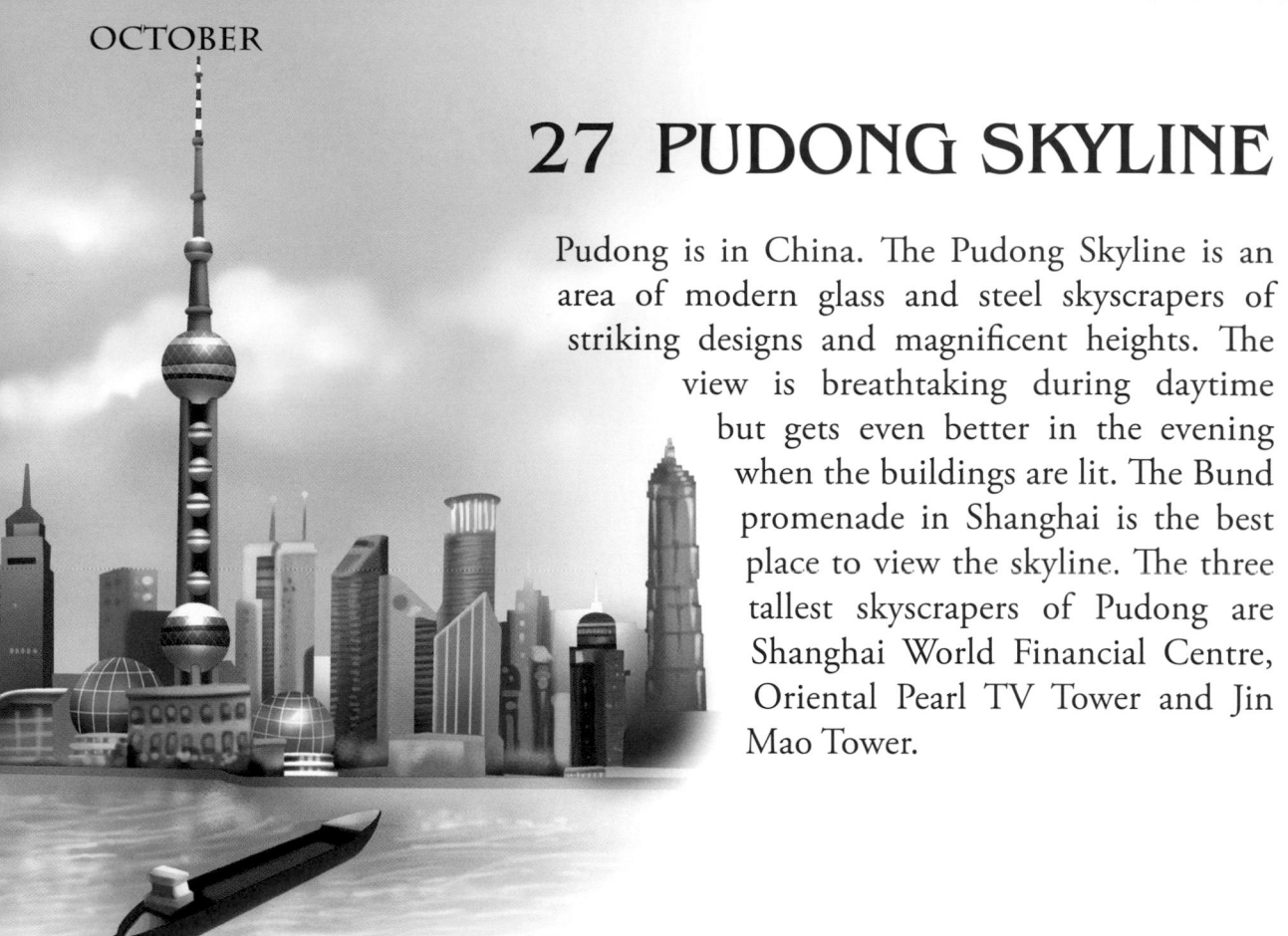

27 PUDONG SKYLINE

Pudong is in China. The Pudong Skyline is an area of modern glass and steel skyscrapers of striking designs and magnificent heights. The view is breathtaking during daytime but gets even better in the evening when the buildings are lit. The Bund promenade in Shanghai is the best place to view the skyline. The three tallest skyscrapers of Pudong are Shanghai World Financial Centre, Oriental Pearl TV Tower and Jin Mao Tower.

28 UA POU

Ua Pou is an island in the Marquesas archipelago, French Polynesia. The name 'Ua Pou' comes from the tall spires that arise from the centre of the mountain. These spires are remnants of ancient volcanoes. Hakahau is the main village of Ua Pou. It has the first Marquesan church which was built in 1859. Ua Pou is famous for wood carvings, tattoos and its musicians and dancers.

29 METEORA

Meteora is in Thessaly, Greece. '*Meteora*' in Greek means 'suspended in midair'. It is famous for the monasteries on top of the rock towers. Today only a few of these remain. The monks settled in these monasteries from the 11th century onwards. One of these monasteries, Saint Stephan, is a nunnery. The Meteora was designated a UNESCO World Heritage Site in 1988.

30 DOGE PALACE

Doge Palace is in Venice, Italy. The leader of the Venetian government was given the title 'Doge'. A doge was elected for life and lived in the palace. After quite a few reconstructions, the Doge Palace steadily altered itself from a crude 9th-century fortress into a graceful 15th-century palace. The top palace attractions are the Grand Council Chamber and the Bridge of Sighs.

31 SALAMANCA OLD TOWN

Salamanca Old Town is in Spain. Some major things to see in the town are the Plaza Mayor, linked cathedrals, University quarter and House of Shells. One of the universities dates back to the early 1200s. This 15th-century House of Shells is decorated on the outside with 350 shells. The Salamanca Old Town was designated a UNESCO World Heritage Site in 1988.

Did You Know?

- Around 1,000 ships used to cross the Panama Canal yearly in its early days. This number has now risen to 14,702 yearly.
- In the 18th century, the site where the Empire State Building stands was the John Thomson Farm where a stream ran across and emptied in Sunfish Pond.
- The Burney Falls have a constant water flow rate of 100 million U.S. gallons a day.

1 PETRA

Petra is an ancient city in Jordan. It is one of the New Seven Wonders of the World. The site consists of tombs, temples and other monumental buildings carved into solid sandstone cliffs. The Nabataeans sculpted the cliff buildings of Petra. The Nabataeans were an Arab tribe that flourished from around the 4th century BC to AD 106. They were extraordinary engineers who constructed a refined pipe-and-tunnel water system to bring in drinking water and keep out flash floods. Some of the major attractions of Petra are the Byzantine Church, Great Temple, Monastery, the Siq and the Treasury. The Byzantine Church dates back to the 5th and 6th centuries and contains some remarkable Byzantine mosaics. The Great Temple is one of the largest structures of Petra and dates back to the 1st century BC. The Siq is a sandstone canyon consisting of Nabatean carvings and monuments. The Treasury is a favourite among the tourists. Petra was designated a UNESCO World Heritage Site in 1985.

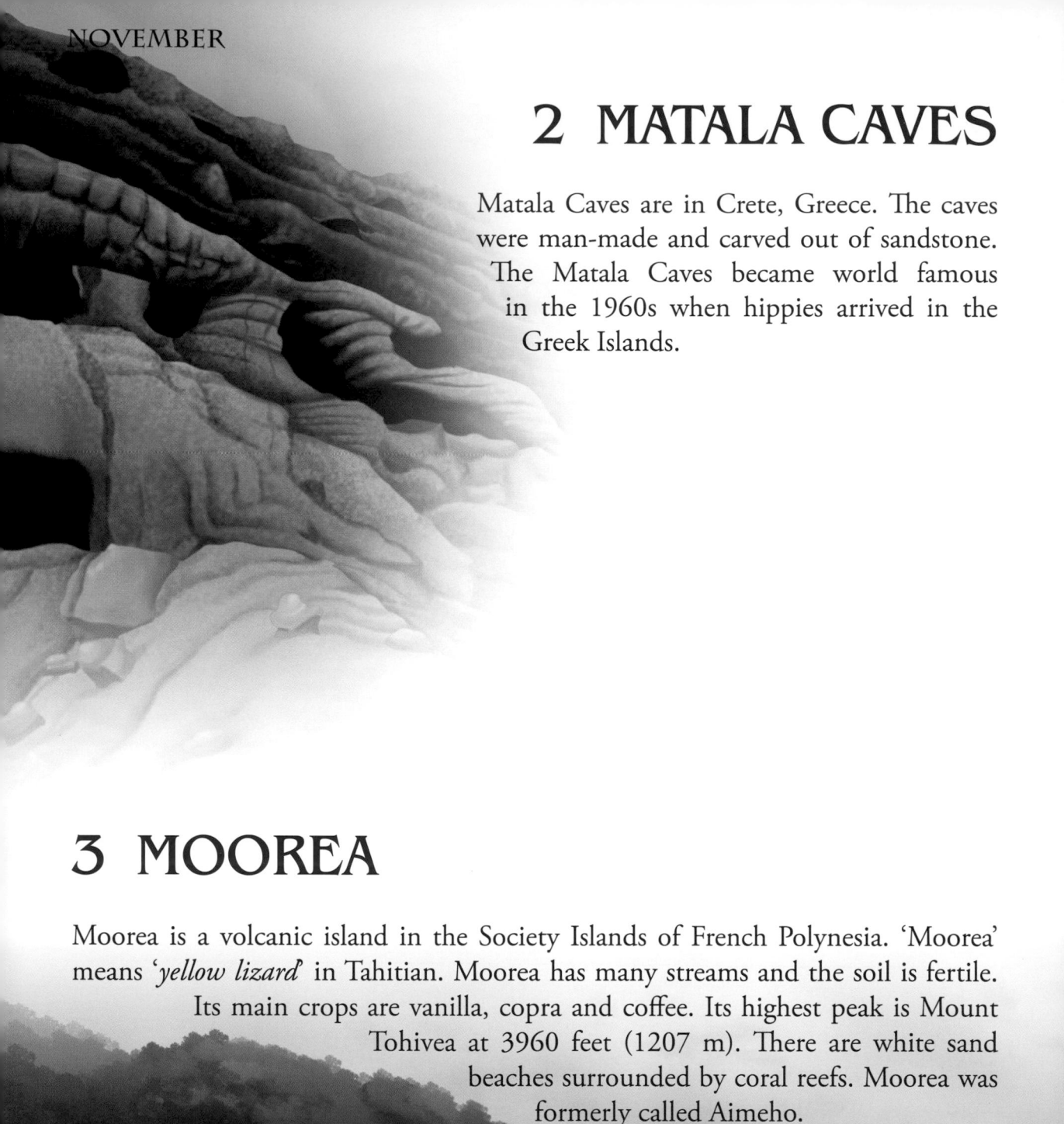

2 MATALA CAVES

Matala Caves are in Crete, Greece. The caves were man-made and carved out of sandstone. The Matala Caves became world famous in the 1960s when hippies arrived in the Greek Islands.

3 MOOREA

Moorea is a volcanic island in the Society Islands of French Polynesia. 'Moorea' means *yellow lizard* in Tahitian. Moorea has many streams and the soil is fertile. Its main crops are vanilla, copra and coffee. Its highest peak is Mount Tohivea at 3960 feet (1207 m). There are white sand beaches surrounded by coral reefs. Moorea was formerly called Aimeho.

4 MYKONOS

Mykonos is a beautiful island in Greece. The island looks just like a postcard with little white houses, hand-painted streets, windmills, pigeon keepers, chimneys and little churches. The place is great for having parties.

5 HERCULANEUM

Herculaneum is an ancient city in Campania, Italy. Herculaneum was buried by the eruption of Mt. Vesuvius in AD 79. The first discovery of ruins was made in 1709. Important early finds were the sumptuous Villa of the Papyri (with a large library, and bronze and marble statues), a basilica with fine murals, and a theatre. The ruins of Herculaneum were designated a UNESCO World Heritage Site in 1997.

6 BURGOS CATHEDRAL

Burgos Cathedral is in Burgos, Spain. It is known for its size and Gothic architecture. It is the main attraction for the tourists. The construction of the cathedral started in 1221 and went on till the 1700s. The cathedral is the burial place of the Spanish national hero El Cid and his widow. The cathedral has over a dozen chapels. The Constable's Chapel is the most well-known.

7 BRYCE CANYON NATIONAL PARK

Bryce Canyon National Park is in Utah, U.S. This area has spectacular rock formations. The canyon was named after Ebenezer Bryce, an early settler in the area. The park was created in 1928. The site has rocks with fantastic shapes formed by erosion known as 'hoodoos'. Various types of wildflowers can be seen here like the bellflower, yarrow, gillia, sego lily and Manzanita.

8 SYDNEY HARBOUR BRIDGE

The Sydney Harbour Bridge is across the Sydney Harbour. It is one of the longest steel-arch bridges in the world. The bridge is nicknamed the 'Coat Hanger' because of its arch-based design. The bridge was opened in 1932. There is a guided tour to the very top of the bridge.

9 TEMPLE OF HEAVEN

The Temple of Heaven is a set of religious buildings in Beijing, China. Its Chinese name is *Tiantan*. The temple was built in the early 15th century and was later renovated and improved several times. It covers 2,700,000 square metres. The temple buildings were used for sacrificial ceremonies and prayers by the emperors of the Ming and Qing Dynasties. The most well known and stunning of the buildings is the House of Prayer for Good Harvest.

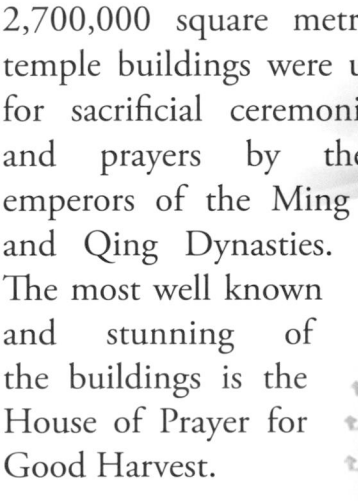

199

10 FATU HIVA

Fatu Hiva is the southernmost of the Marquesas Islands in French Polynesia. The Bay of Virgins is a hotspot of Fatu Hiva. The people here are good at wood carvings. They also specialise in making topa (beaten bark painted with elaborate drawings).

11 SAMARIA GORGE

The Samaria Gorge is in Crete, Greece. People can enjoy hiking here. One can walk 16 kilometres (11 miles) while descending 1250 metres (4100 ft). The best part of the hike is passing through the Portes. The opening of the Portes narrows to about 3.5 metres (12 ft).

12 ITALIAN LAKE DISTRICT

Italian Lake District is in Italy. Bordered by grand snow-capped mountains, the district is one of the most romantic places in Italy. The hillsides are covered with olive groves, lemon and banana trees. Flowers like rhododendrons, azaleas and camellias grow here. Lakes Maggiore and Como are very popular among tourists. The lakes were carved by glaciers.

13 EL ESCORIAL

El Escorial is in Madrid, Spain. The building contains a royal pantheon, palace, monastery, basilica, library, school and art collection. Escorial has 9 towers, 16 patios, 73 statues, 86 sets of stairs, 88 fountains, 300 cells, 1200 windows, 2673 doors, and more than 1600 paintings. Some things to see in El Escorial are the Royal Crypt, Basilica, Library, Art Galleries and Philip II Chambers.

14 HAWAII VOLCANOES NATIONAL PARK

Hawaii Volcanoes National Park is in Hawaii. The park has two of the most active volcanoes in the world, Mauna Loa (4170 m) and Kilauea (1250 m). Rare birds and endemic species can be found in the national park area. The park was designated a UNESCO World Heritage Site in 1987.

15 THREE GORGES DAM

Three Gorges Dam is in China. It is the world's largest dam. The dam measures 185 metres (610 ft). high and 2.3 kilometres (1.3 miles) wide. The Three Gorges Dam is a 15-year project. The cost is about US $30 billion.

16 LINDOS ACROPOLIS

Lindos Acropolis is in Greece. It is a very popular tourist attraction. The word 'acropolis' means *'high city'* in Greek. The Temple of Athena is the most famous building. The Acropolis has a vast complex of structures of different styles. These include Classical Greek, Hellenistic, Roman and Byzantine.

17 MILAN CATHEDRAL

Milan Cathedral is in Milan, Italy. The cathedral dates back to the 14th century and took 500 years to complete. The tallest spire of the cathedral is crowned with the Madonnina statue, 100 metres above street level. The cathedral can accommodate up to 40,000 people.

18 GAUDI SACRED FAMILY CHURCH

Gaudi Sacred Family Church is in Barcelona, Spain. The construction of the church began in 1883 and is still incomplete. There were many reasons for the delay in construction. For example, the Spanish Civil War. Gaudi designed the church. The church is Barcelona's most famous tourist attraction.

19 MUSEUM OF MODERN ART

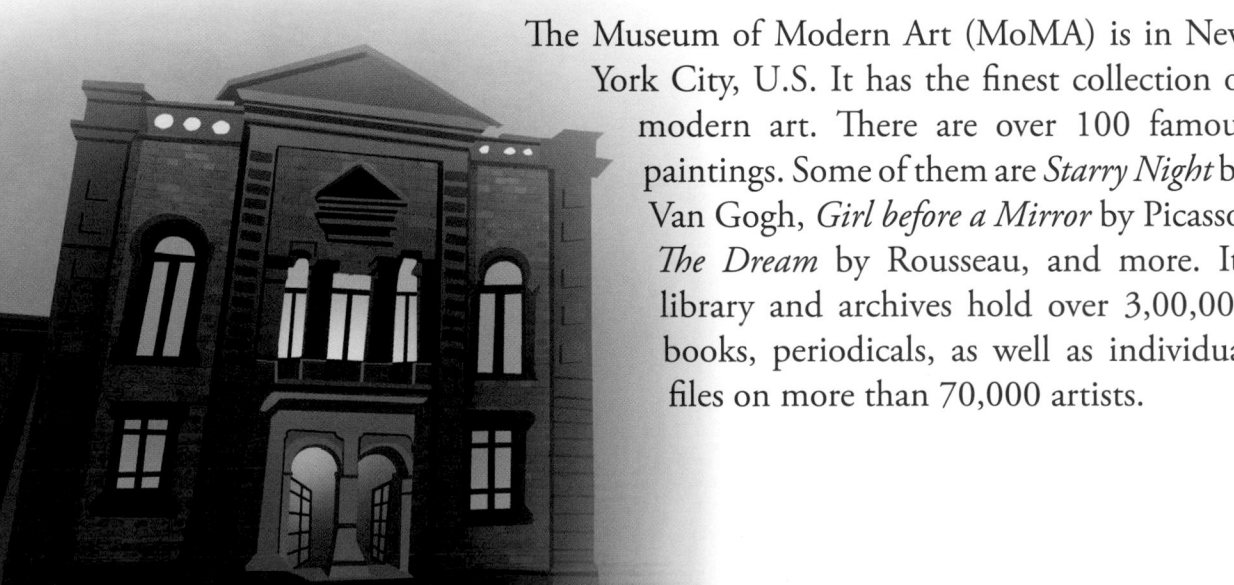

The Museum of Modern Art (MoMA) is in New York City, U.S. It has the finest collection of modern art. There are over 100 famous paintings. Some of them are *Starry Night* by Van Gogh, *Girl before a Mirror* by Picasso, *The Dream* by Rousseau, and more. Its library and archives hold over 3,00,000 books, periodicals, as well as individual files on more than 70,000 artists.

20 TIGER LEAPING GORGE

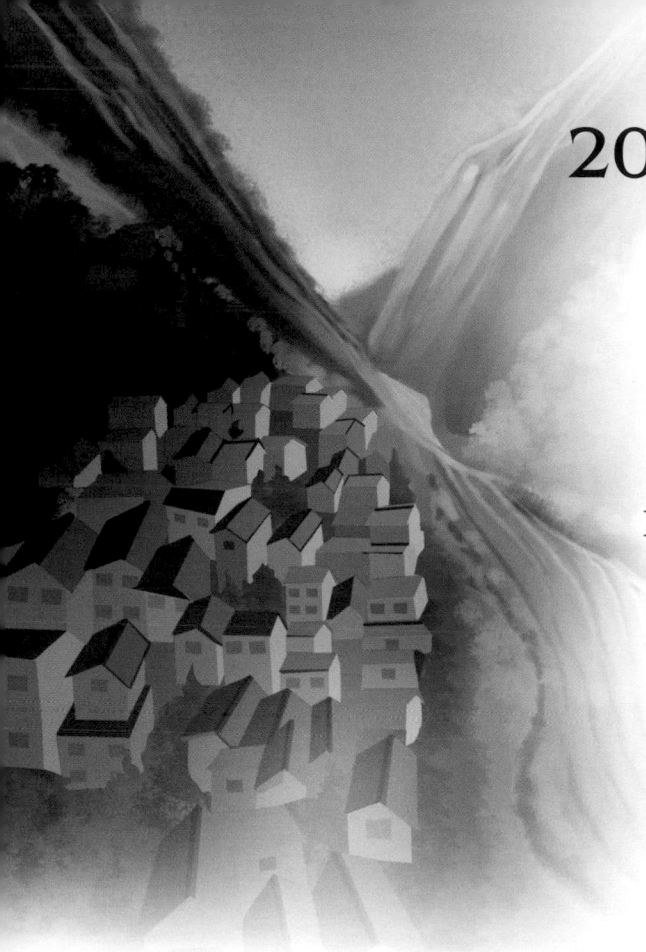

The Tiger Leaping Gorge is in China. According to legend, a tiger escaped a hunter by jumping over the gorge, hence the name. The gorge is called *Hutiao* in Chinese. It is 15 kilometres (9 miles) long. There are mountains on both sides of the gorge.

21 PAROS

Paros is an island in Greece. It has lovely beaches, white-washed houses and a lively nightlife. It is famous for its perfect weather conditions for windsurfing. Paros is the third-largest island of the Cyclades, after Naxos and Andros, with a surface area of 186 square kilometres and 120 kilometres of coastline.

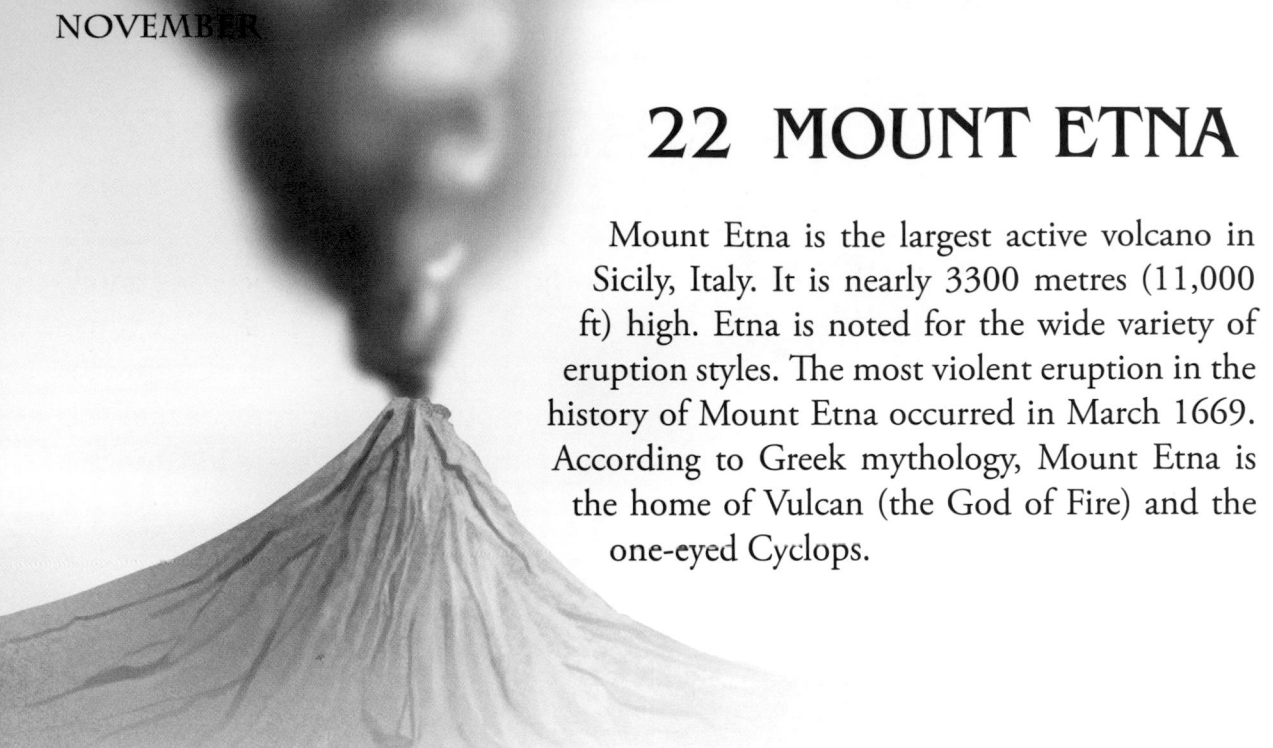

22 MOUNT ETNA

Mount Etna is the largest active volcano in Sicily, Italy. It is nearly 3300 metres (11,000 ft) high. Etna is noted for the wide variety of eruption styles. The most violent eruption in the history of Mount Etna occurred in March 1669. According to Greek mythology, Mount Etna is the home of Vulcan (the God of Fire) and the one-eyed Cyclops.

23 PAMPLONA

Pamplona is in Spain. The famous bull running festival, known as Encierro, takes place here. It is a huge draw for tourists. The festival begins with rocket firing. The bulls are made to run across the town with adventurous people trying to dodge their deadly horns.

24 ALASKA CRUISE

On an Alaska Cruise, one passes the fjords lined with glaciers and snow-capped sharp peaks. The two most popular cruises are the Inland Passage cruise and the Gulf of Alaska cruise. The Inland Passage cruise consists of a 7-day round trip out of Vancouver, B.C. (or Seattle, Washington) to the Inland Passage to see its fjords, glaciers and towns. Some of the highlights of the Inland Passage cruise are Glacier Bay National Park, College Fjord and Skagway. The Gulf of Alaska cruise has the Inland Passage cruise as well as a visit to the glaciers farther north.

25 RHODES OLD TOWN

Rhodes Old Town is in Greece. The topmost feature of the town is the Palace of the Grandmaster. It was the headquarters of the Knights of St. John. Its walls are 4 kilometres (2.5 miles) long. The walls surround both the palace and the town. Other important places include the Great Hospital and the Street of the Knights. The old town was designated a UNESCO World Heritage Site in 1988.

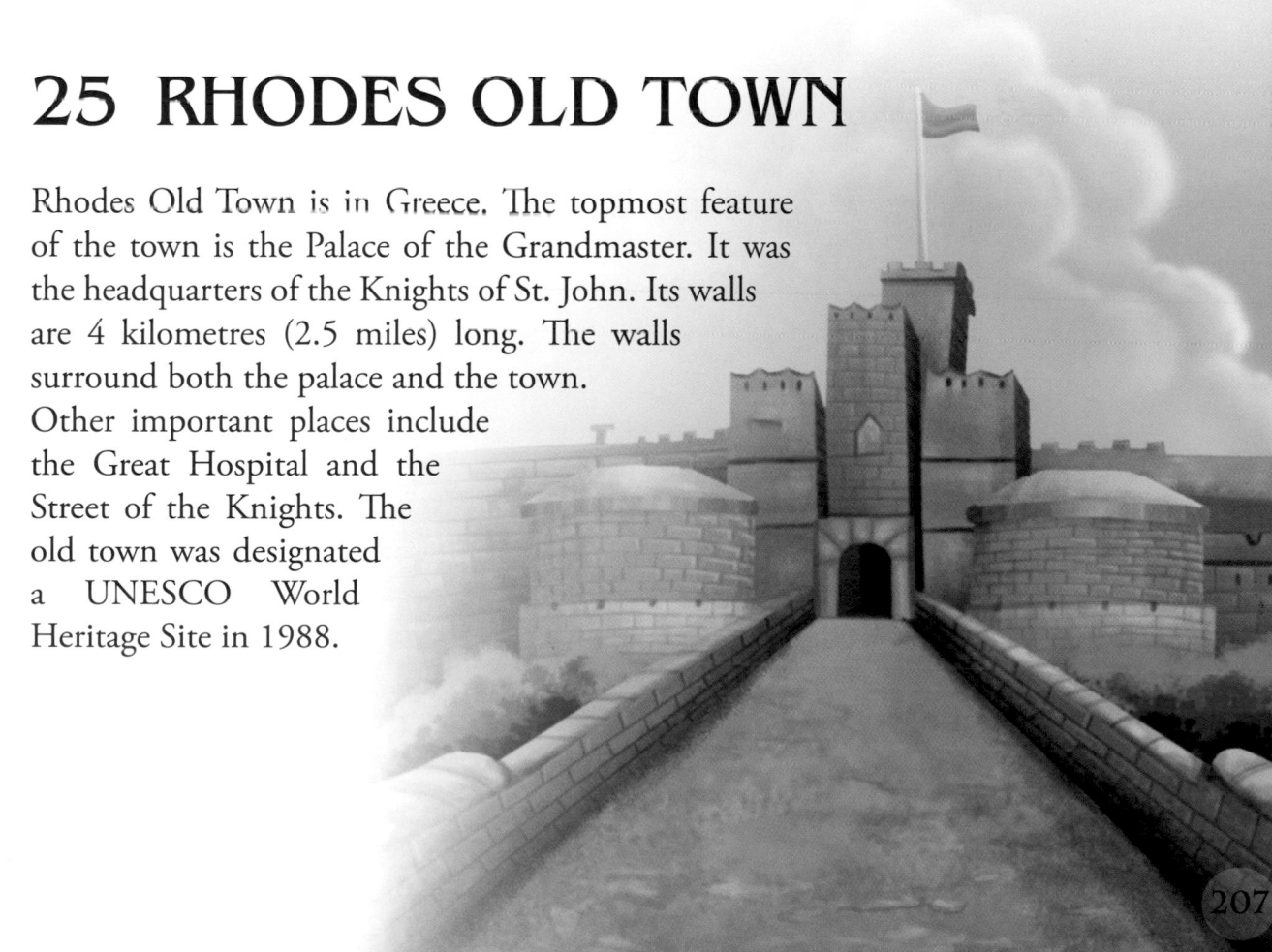

26 PAESTUM

Paestum is an ancient city in southern Italy. Its main highlight is the three Doric temples; Apollo, Ceres and Hera. They are well preserved despite being 2500 years old. Apollo is also called the Temple of Neptune. Ceres is called the Temple of Athena and Hera is known as the Basilica. Apollo is the best preserved of the three.

27 PRADO MUSEUM

The Prado Museum is an art museum in Madrid, Spain. The museum holds an excellent collection of European paintings from the 12th to the 19th centuries. The museum houses masterpieces by Titian, Bosch, Botticelli, Rembrandt, Fra Angelico, El Greco, Velázquez, Francisco de Goya, José de Ribera, Francisco de Zurbarán Hiëronymus Bosch, Pieter Bruegel the Elder, Raphael, Tintoretto, Paolo Veronese, Peter Paul Rubens, Anthony Van Dyck, Nicolas Poussin, Claude Lorrain and Antoine Watteau.

28 NATIONAL ARCHAEOLOGICAL MUSEUM

The National Archaeological Museum is in Athens, Greece. It is the largest museum in Greece and also one of the most important museums in the world containing ancient Greek art. The museum houses sculptures, bronzes, pottery, jewellery and artifacts from all parts of Greece. The highlight of the main museum is *La Dama de Elche* (Lady of Elx in English), the bust of a wealthy 5th-century BC Iberian woman.

29 PITTI PALACE

The Pitti Palace is in Florence, Italy. The Pitti Palace houses some of the most important museums in Florence. The palace and the Boboli gardens house the Palatine Gallery, the Silver Museum, the Museum of Modern Art, the Costume Gallery, the Porcelain Museum and the Museum of Carriages.

30 ROYAL PALACE

The Royal Palace is in Madrid, Spain. It is also called *Palacio Real* in Spanish. The palace dates back to the 18th century and features beautiful artwork. The Royal Palace is the official residence of the current king but he does not live there. The palace is however used as a museum. It has 870 windows, 240 balconies, 44 sets of stairs and 110 doors. The palace houses a huge collection of classical Spanish artwork by Goya and Velázquez.

Did You Know?

- Over 7,00,000 workers were employed to build the Terracotta Army of Qin Shi Huang, the first emperor of China.
- The Stonehenge in the English county of Wiltshire served as a burial ground for at least 500 years.
- The Porcelain Tower of Nanjing is also known to the Chinese as Bao'ensi, which means 'Temple of Gratitude'.

1 SYDNEY OPERA HOUSE

The Sydney Opera House is in Sydney, Australia. It is one of the most famous performing art centres in the world. It was completed in 1973. The opera house was conceived and built by Danish architect Jorn Utzon. It has a unique architectural design. The opera house is more than an opera house. It is a performing arts complex with a 2680-seat concert hall and a 1550-seat venue for opera. There are playhouses and studios inside the Opera House as well. There are many bars and restaurants in the opera house. A wide range of performances are staged, including symphonic music, opera, theatre and ballet. It was designated a UNESCO World Heritage Site in 2007.

2 OLYMPIA

Olympia is a ruined sanctuary of Greece. It was the home of the ancient Olympic Games. It was designated a UNESCO World Heritage site in 1989. Olympia contained many treasures of Greek art, such as temples, monuments, altars, theatres, statues and votive offerings of brass and marble. The Temple of Zeus was the largest and most important building at Olympia.

3 ROMAN FORUM

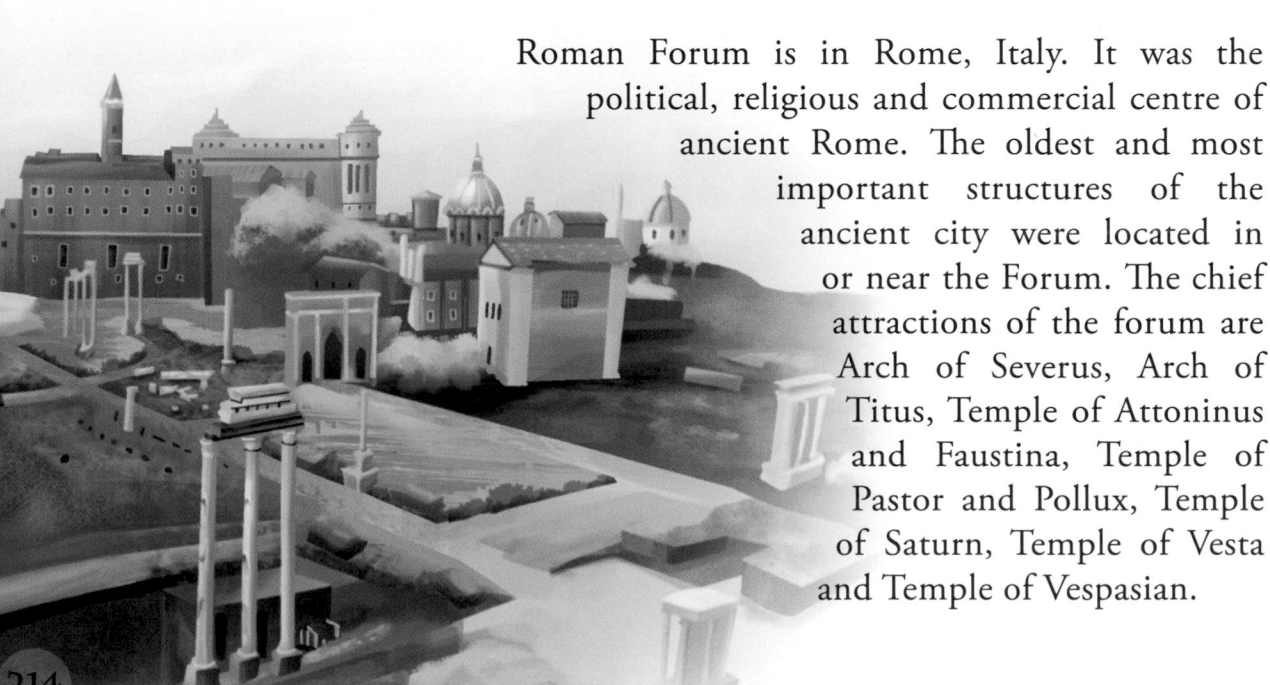

Roman Forum is in Rome, Italy. It was the political, religious and commercial centre of ancient Rome. The oldest and most important structures of the ancient city were located in or near the Forum. The chief attractions of the forum are Arch of Severus, Arch of Titus, Temple of Attoninus and Faustina, Temple of Pastor and Pollux, Temple of Saturn, Temple of Vesta and Temple of Vespasian.

4 SANTIAGO DE COMPOSTELA

Santiago de Compostela is in Spain. There is a 12th-century cathedral in Santiago de Compostela that is very famous. The tomb of the cathedral supposedly holds the remains of St. James. The city's route was proclaimed the first European Cultural Itinerary by the Council of Europe in 1987. There are around 1800 historical buildings, both religious and secular, along the route.

5 METROPOLITAN MUSEUM OF ART

The Metropolitan Museum of Art is in New York City, U.S. It is also known as the Met. It has a collection of more than two million works of art. It is considered one of the world's two greatest all-around art museums. The collection has pieces that are over 5000 years old. The museum has a collection of American, European, Egyptian, Greek and Roman art.

6 TEMPLE OF POSEIDON

The Temple of Poseidon is located in Cape Sounion, Greece. It offers a wide view of the sea and the close by Greek Islands. The temple was constructed in 440 BC. It was built to honour Poseidon, the Greek God of the Sea. Local marble was used for the temple's Doric columns. Of the 34, only 15 survive today.

7 SAN GIMIGNANO

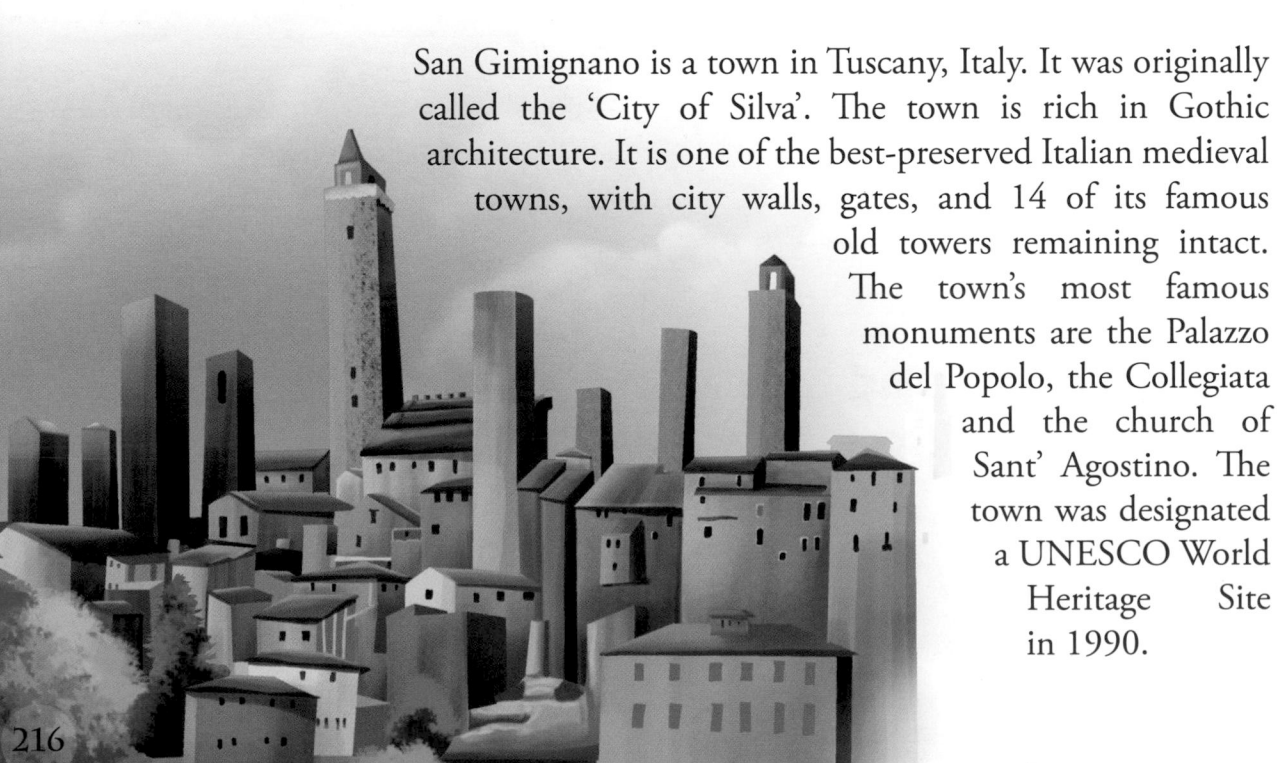

San Gimignano is a town in Tuscany, Italy. It was originally called the 'City of Silva'. The town is rich in Gothic architecture. It is one of the best-preserved Italian medieval towns, with city walls, gates, and 14 of its famous old towers remaining intact. The town's most famous monuments are the Palazzo del Popolo, the Collegiata and the church of Sant' Agostino. The town was designated a UNESCO World Heritage Site in 1990.

8 AVILA WALLS

Avila is in Spain. It is famous for its magnificent walls that surround the city. They are among the longest and best-preserved walls in the world. They were built in the 11th and 12th centuries. The walls are 2.5 kilometres (1.5 mile) long, 12 metres (40 ft) high and 3 metres (10 ft) thick. There are 88 towers and nine gates.

9 ROMANTIC ROAD

The Romantic Road is in Bavaria, Germany. The road takes us through a variety of walled medieval towns, eye-catching castles, and unspoiled countryside in Bavaria. The road starts from Wurzburg and ends at Fussen. The route is also known for passing by the famous Neuschwanstein Castle. Between Wurzburg and Fussen is a town called Rothenburg.

10 HAWAIIAN ISLANDS

The Hawaiian Islands are in the United States. These green volcanic islands have white sand beaches and an agreeable climate. The best resort islands are Kauai, Lanai and Maui. The islands' have coral reefs, colourful fish and the green sea turtles. Each island has its own characteristic features attracting tourists from all over.

11 TUSCAN COUNTRYSIDE

Tuscany is in Italy. It has one of the world's most picturesque countryside. There are medieval villages, castle ruins and old farmhouses. The slopes have vineyards and olive groves. The most beautiful countryside lies between Siena and Florence. The most interesting small hilltop villages are Pienza, Montepulciano and San Biagio.

12 GOTHIC QUARTER

The Gothic Quarter is in Barcelona, Spain. It is called so because there are many Gothic structures that rose in the 13th to 15th centuries. Cathedral de la Seu is the highlight of the Gothic Quarter. Other than the cathedral, there are the former Royal Palace and the Picasso Museum. The palace has the sculpture-rich Frederic-Mares Museum. There are many antique shops in the quarter.

13 VILLA D'ESTE

The Villa d'Este is at Tivoli, Italy. With its palace and garden, it is one of the most remarkable and comprehensive illustrations of Renaissance culture. There are about 500 fountains in the villa. Some things to see are the Organ Fountain, Hundred Fountains, Neptune Fountain, Oval Fountain and Dragon Fountain. In the Organ Fountain, music is heard as the water comes out of the pipes. It was designated a UNESCO World Heritage Site in 2001.

14 COSTA DEL SOL

The Costa del Sol is in Spain. It is one of Spain's most popular tourist destinations. Beaches, golf and celebrities are the highlights of Costa del Sol. The place has the largest number of golf clubs in entire Europe. There are sandy beaches, night clubs, restaurants, etc. Some popular tourist towns are Marbella, Puerto Banus, Torremolinos, Benalmad and Fuengirola.

15 SAINT PETER'S SQUARE

Saint Peter's Square is in the Vatican City, Rome. It is 240 metres wide. The square was constructed in the middle of the 17th century. It was designed by Gian Lorenzo Bernini. The style is baroque. The square is made up of two different areas. The first has a trapezoid shape and the second is elliptical. The square is used for public masses and ceremonies.

16 CUENCA OLD TOWN

Cuenca Old Town is in central Spain. The town is perched on a rock formation sided by the gorges of two rivers. It is famous for its hanging houses. The houses date back to the 14th and 15th centuries. There are lovely pastel coloured-buildings and cobblestone streets. There is also a Museum of Spanish Abstract that attracts many a tourist.

17 VATICAN MUSEUMS

The Vatican Museums are located inside the Vatican City. There are paintings, sculptures and other artworks collected by the popes through the centuries. The museums include several architectural marvels such as the Sistine Chapel, the Chapel of Beato Angelico, the Raphael Rooms, the Loggia and the Borgia Apartment. The north end has the Pio-Clementino Museum, Egyptian Museum, Etruscan Museum and Vatican Picture Gallery. The south end contains the Raphael Rooms, Borgia Apartments and Sistine Chapel.

18 IBIZA

Ibiza is an island in Spain. The island was of great importance in ancient times and was inhabited by the Phoenicians and the Carthaginians. The island is well-known for its parties. It has some notable archaeological sites. Ibiza is often called the White Island for its typical architecture. Dry fruits like almonds, dried figs and apricots are exported. Tourism is the main trade of Ibiza.

19 CASTEL SANT'ANGELO

Castel Sant'Angelo is in Rome, Italy. During the 2nd century BC it was constructed as a tomb for Emperor Hadrian. During the mid-6th century AD the building was converted into a fortress and became the military fortress. In 1901, it was converted into a museum. It got its name from the statue of the archangel Michael that crowns the building. The building has a great design.

20 TOLEDO OLD TOWN

Toledo Old Town is in Spain. Christians, Jews and Muslims have largely lived in harmony in the town for many centuries. There is an Alcazar fortress, a 13th century Gothic cathedral and a medieval maze of narrow, twisting and cobblestone streets in the town. The cathedral has a collection of art by Goya, El Greco and other masters.

21 MOUNT VESUVIUS

Mount Vesuvius is a volcano on the western coast of Italy. It is the famous volcano which destroyed Pompeii and other towns of Rome in AD 79. The volcano stands about 1300 metres (4200 ft) above sea level. One can see vineyards on the slopes of the volcano. Lachryma Christi is widely known.

22 PIAZZA DELLA SIGNORIA

The Piazza della Signoria is in Florence, Italy and dates back to the 13th century. Some of the original buildings have disappeared but still it retains its beauty. The piazza is surrounded by many other important buildings like the Loggia della Signoria and the Palazzo degli Uffizi on the south side, the Palazzo degli Uguccioni on the north side and the Palazzo del Tribunale di Mercanzia on the east side.

23 POSITANO

Positano is a small town in Italy. It is considered one of the most beautiful and picturesque places of the world. The small houses, beaches and the friendliness of the people lend it a great charm. The houses are covered with bougainvillea flowers. Positano has a lot of steep steps winding through a maze of narrow passageways.

24 ST. MARK'S SQUARE

St. Mark's Square is in Venice, Italy. It dates back to the 9th century. There are several architectural marvels including the St. Mark's Basilica. St. Mark's square is defined by arcades on three sides and St. Mark's church on the eastern end. One thing that can't be missed is the pigeons. They are everywhere. The square has always been the location of important government buildings.

25 SYRACUSE

Syracuse is in Sicily. The city is built on an ancient Greek settlement founded by Corinthians in 734 BC. Syracuse was home to famous people like Archimedes, Pindar and Aeschylus. It was one of the most important cities in Greece with a population of around 3,00,000. It once rivalled Athens in importance.

26 SIENA

Siena is a city in Tuscany, Italy. It was an important commercial and banking city until surpassed by Florence in the 13th–14th century. The shell-shaped square, Piazza del Campo, is the heart of Siena. Piazza del Campo is best known for being the location of the Palio, one of the world's most thrilling horse races. Other places to see are the Duomo, Pinacoteca and the streets. Pinacoteca is a museum that has many Renaissance paintings. The historic centre of Siena has been designated a UNESCO World Heritage Site in 1995.

27 SPANISH STEPS

The Spanish Steps are in Rome, Italy. The steps date back to the 18th century. The steps connect the Piazza di Spagna at the base and Piazza Trinità dei Monti above. The steps are one of the world's most popular gathering places for tourists. The steps were named after the Spanish Embassy for the Vatican. They were designed by Francesco de Sanctis and were built between 1723 and 1726.

28 TAORMINA

Taormina is in Sicily, Italy. The town overlooks the Mediterranean sea. The main attraction is its Amphitheatre. The amphitheatre is on a high hill with a great view of the town. One can also see Mt. Etna from here. The mixture of scenic beauty and moderate climatic conditions has made Taormina a well-known tourist resort. Despite the number of tourists coming to Taormina, it has retained its ambiance.

29 PIAZZA DEL DUOMO

Piazza del Duomo is in Florence, Italy. It holds a beautiful collection of architectural riches. These riches go back to the 13th century. There are three important parts of the piazza: Baptistry, Cathedral and Belltower. Baptistry is Battistero, Cathedral is Duomo and Belltower is Campanile in Italian. The Duomo is one of the world's largest cathedrals and was begun in 1296. Campanile dates back to the 1300s and is 85 metres (280 ft). Piazza del Duomo was designated a UNESCO World Heritage Site in 1987.

30 VERDON CANYON

Verdon Canyon is in France. It is also known as Verdon Gorge or the Grand Canyon of Verdon. The canyon was chiselled through the limestone rock over millions of years by the region's river. The prime stretch is 21 kilometres (13 miles) long and up to 700 metres (2300 ft) deep.

31 SANTA MARIA DELLE GRAZIE

Santa Maria delle Grazie is a church in Milan, Italy. It is famous because it houses the most well-known painting in the world, *The Last Supper* by Leonardo da Vinci. The painting shows Jesus with his 12 apostles. The painting was begun in 1495 and was painted on a plastered wall in the church. It is 8.8 metres (29 ft) wide by 4.6 metres (15 ft) high. Santa Maria delle Grazie is designated a UNESCO World Heritage Site in 1980.

Index

OTHER TITLES IN THIS SERIES

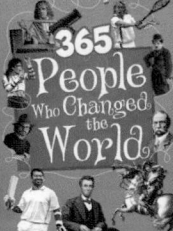

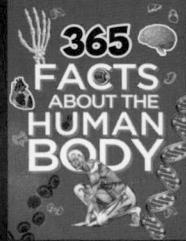